Pleasant Places:
a tribute to the Gower ministry
of the Rev. B. Tudor Lloyd

i Megan, gyda phob dymuniad da
i chi a'n teulu. Mae gennyf llawer
o atgofion melys o'n amser yn
y Tabernacl, ac oddi ar hynny,

Tudor

Benjamin Tudor Lloyd: Graduation at Cambridge 1956.

Pleasant Places:
a tribute to the Gower ministry of the Rev. B. Tudor Lloyd

Edited by
Eifion Evans

Gower Presbyterian Churches

Published by Gower Presbyterian Churches
in association with Llanrhidian History Group

Preface and editorial matter © Eifion Evans 2006
Each essay © the individual contributor 2006

First published 2006

ISBN 0-9547450-3-5

Printed in Wales at
Dinefwr Press, Llandybie, Carmarthenshire

Contents

List of Contributors, and Acknowledgements

Contributors

David Boorman is an elder at Tabernacle, Pen-clawdd.

Eifion Evans is a retired Presbyterian minister and author.

Jonathan I. Hodgins is a Presbyterian Church Community Worker in Gower.

Iain B. Hodgins is minister of the Gower Presbyterian churches.

Eleanor Jenkins is an elder at Bethesda, Burry Green.

Acknowledgements

Gower Presbyterian Churches gratefully acknowledge help from the following:

Gower Society and Llanrhidian History Group for their support in this project.

The staff at the National Library of Wales and Swansea Central Public Library.

The Banner of Truth Trust, for permission to reproduce in Chapter 3 'A map of the part of Wales connected with the early life of Howell Harris', drawn by L. F. Lupton and published in *The Early Life of Howell Harris* in 1962; and the photograph in Chapter 5 of D. Martyn Lloyd-Jones in conversation with John Stott at the Evangelical Alliance meeting, October 18, 1966, from Iain H. Murray, *David Martyn Lloyd-Jones: The Fight of Faith 1939-1981*, Edinburgh, 1990.

The Historical Society of the Presbyterian Church of Wales, for permission to republish from its *Journal*, 21 (1997), 66-91, the lecture on 'William Griffiths (1788-1861) Apostle of Gower', by B. Tudor Lloyd.

The St. Mathias Press, now The Good Book Company, for permission to quote two verses from the Rev. Christopher Idle's hymn in *Light Upon the River*.

Mr. Bryan Belcher.
Mr. Phil Boorman.
The Rev. J. E. Wynne Davies.
Dr. David Gill.
Mr. Peter Griffiths, great, great grandson of William Griffiths.
Mr. Peter S. Jones, Gower Photographic Studios.
Mr. Gruffydd (Ion) Thomas.
Mrs. Pat Williams.

The photograph of the Welsh IVF Conference at Borth, Aberystwyth, in 1951 was taken by Pickfords & Sons, Photographers, Aberystwyth.

Foreword

'I devoted myself', said the Teacher in the book of Ecclesiastes, 'to study and to explore by wisdom all that is done under heaven'. What was the result of that exploration? The declaration that everything is meaningless. What happens in time can not be understood by tracing patterns through time; what happens in history can not be understood by discovering some law that operates within history. And so the Teacher is driven to a conclusion: it is neither time nor history that disclose to us the meaning of our life and labours. It is God and obedience to God that gives them their meaning. We are being pointed in the direction of faith.

The contributions brought together in this volume are a testimony to the power of faith; better, to the power of the One in whom we place our faith. They are a testimony to which we must give heed precisely because we cannot easily understand the times in which we live by trying to discern a pattern. Yet countless single-minded men and women, some better and some less well-known, crowd the pages of this volume and bear witness to the one thing that is needful. We are invited to learn about a fragment of the story of the work of God in Gower over the decades and centuries: a divine activity and a human chain; a divine power and a human dedication; a divine grace and a human response. It is the story of a church animated by the power of the Spirit.

Stories such as these can be told either with starry-eyed romanticism or with dry-eyed indifference. The contributors go to neither extreme; they are united in their joy over the past, sorrow over the present and hope for the future. All three attitudes must surely indwell our hearts in equal measure where their object is the one work of God and the Gospel. When they are separated, we lapse into escapism, despondency or false optimism. When they are joined, we become determined, sober and faithful.

This book is produced to mark Tudor Lloyd's completion of fifty years in ordained ministry. We learn much about him that is unexpected; not many ministers in the Calvinistic Methodist Connexion have the ability to bring two-year-old girls to tears by an unfortunate drawing of a cat! But, in addition to having the facts of his life and ministry described to us, we also learn what we expected; Tudor Lloyd has been a faithful witness to his Lord day in, day out, year in, year out on the Peninsula, standing in the succession of leaders that have sought to bring Christ and his Word to the congregations. We know, as Paul tells the Corinthians, that his labour in the Lord has not been in vain. For his deep integrity and constant faithfulness, we give thanks to God. It is my privilege to express my personal admiration and gratitude as I warmly commend this volume to everyone who desires to see the Gospel flourish in Gower, in every denomination, and throughout the land of Wales.

Stephen N. Williams
Belfast
May, 2006

Preface

In life's wider context the year 1956, a mere 50 years ago, might be remembered for a variety of reasons. It saw the conflict that became known as 'The Suez Crisis', the development of an oral vaccine against polio, and the emergence of Elvis Presley as an international pop star. For Gower the year marked its designation as the first Area of Outstanding Natural Beauty in the United Kingdom, a thoroughly deserved recognition of so many distinguished features compressed into so few geographical miles. It was also the year in which a Presbyterian Pastorate welcomed a new minister in the person of the newly ordained B. Tudor Lloyd, commencing a ministry in Gower that has made a significant spiritual contribution to the lives of many. This book seeks to celebrate that achievement with thanksgiving to God on their behalf.

To speak, as the title sets out, of *Pleasant Places*, is to use the biblical language of Psalm 16:6, and it is intended to convey not only congenial surroundings but also, as the verse continues, a goodly spiritual heritage both bestowed and bequeathed. In this respect the title reflects Mr. Lloyd's ministry, and the book's contributors have sought to be faithful to this portrayal. In addition, *Pleasant Places* is a phrase that acknowledges the several locations in which that ministry was exercised, where people made up churches for Christian worship, witness and work. This is why the chapter titles use the imagery of a building, drawn from Scripture, and sets out important elements of structure and habitation. After all, as the Apostle Peter reminds us, Christian are 'like living stones . . . being built up as a spiritual house' (1 Pet. 2:5).

The book begins with a tribute to Mr. Lloyd as a wise 'masterbuilder' under God, while at the same time defining the evangelical Christianity which he promoted. He was following in the tradition of early nonconformity in Gower when its witness to the Gospel must have seemed to be a mere 'heap of stones', with hardly the promise of a lasting presence. Then came the fiery evangelism of Calvinistic Methodists like Howel Harris, which unashamedly aimed 'to set up the house of our God' by preaching, and consolidation through fellowship meetings. In another generation, Lady Barham's religious zeal aided the work, finding in William Griffths a minister whose labours were 'apostolic' in their pioneering spirit. By the end of the nineteenth century, foundations had been 'strongly laid', foundations which in the last century were shaken by 'contrary winds' and 'tensions', but 'the house did not fall'. To this day in Gower there are, consequently, 'houses full of good things', and not least among them are the churches of the Presbyterian pastorate, whose members in the closing sections of the book acknowledge with fondness and gratitude. It is fitting that the present minister, Iain B. Hodgins, closes this tribute with an affirmation of prospect and intention, 'to rebuild the house' that his predecessor laboured so diligently to preserve.

The contributors have worked as a team, to the admiration of a grateful editor. The Pastorate, as the book's publisher, is grateful to Professor Williams for his 'Foreword', which stems from an affectionate link between his father and Mr. Lloyd. The sources used, acknowledgments for help and for permission to use material, appear at the end of the book. The first Appendix provides the reader with the story of William Griffiths, originally delivered as a lecture by Mr. Lloyd. In publishing the book, members of the Pastorate rejoice in the power of God's Gospel in their midst, and dedicate it to God's glory.

1. 'A wise master-builder'

Iain B. Hodgins

Every man is to a great extent the product of his inheritance –
John R. W. Stott

The Singing Group were making their way to an engagement in Pontardawe when they noticed a familiar figure waiting at the bus stop. "Come with us, May", they called. Being in two minds about abandoning her intention of going to Sunday School, she followed them into the Workhouse. The singers knew what an asset May Protheroe's voice would be, since everybody knew that her uncle was the composer, Daniel Protheroe of Cwmgiedd,

now prominent amongst the American Welsh fraternity. She had not only inherited some of his musical capabilities, but shared a number of his spiritual qualities too. Some years earlier, when the Swansea to Brecon Canal had burst its banks, bystanders, knowing that Dan was such a prayerful lad, spontaneously shouted, "send for little Danny to pray for us". That readiness to pray for individuals and their needs is a grace that his great nephew, Tudor, has practiced in public, but especially in secret.

Dr Daniel Protheroe (1866-1934): 'Cerddor, Eisteddfodwr, Gwladgarwr'.

The young Clerk to the Guardians of the Workhouse sitting on the edge of the stage sensed May's worth as a potential life partner that afternoon, and quickly invited her home to tea. From

Tudor in his mother's arms
at Pontardawe.

Tudor with his father
at Porthcawl.

there they went on to the service at Soar Calvinistic Methodist [C.M.] Chapel, Pontardawe, where Richard Lloyd's father and grandfather before him had been Church Secretary. By 1928 Richard and May were married in Pontardawe where they set up home in Dan y Bryn opposite the Workhouse. There, on 28th April 1929 Benjamin Tudor Lloyd was born, sixty-eight years to the day that William Griffiths preached his last sermon "by the door" of Bethesda Chapel, Burry Green! An early photograph shows the baby straining in his mother's arms to reach for his father on his return from work. It was King George VI who used to talk about his family as "we four", and until his father's death in 1980, the Lloyds were very much "we three".

Whilst the Wall Street Crash and continuing effects of the world-wide economic Depression of the time left many dispirited, for Richard Lloyd and his family these were exciting days as they were planning a new life in Cardiff where Richard had secured a new job at County Hall. Typically of the time, Richard and May Lloyd immediately took their letters of transfer to Crwys Road Welsh C.M. Chapel where their son became known as Tudur Llwyd. By his fourth birthday, the family decided to move to an expanding area of Cardiff, where new houses were being built in Whitchurch, but not before Tudor had got his head stuck in the railings of his old home in Inverness Place, where he had to be cut free by the fire brigade!

Now settled at 29 Manor Way the family decided to begin attending the Tabernacle C.M. Chapel, Whitchurch, whose minister was the dignified Rev. John Viner, known as 'the Bishop' and for his rigid time keeping. The Lloyds noticed that although the services at the Tabernacle were conducted in English, the informal conversation afterwards was mainly in Welsh, whereas in the Welsh Chapel at Crwys worship took place in Welsh, but the people conversed in English. Serving as he did for his entire ministry in the English speaking Association of the Presbyterian Church of Wales, many people do not think of Tudor as a Welsh speaker. Those early influences in chapel helped the development of his bilingualism. Being fluent he was in a position to serve as Minute Secretary of the Church's General Assembly in the new millennium, and over the years to carry on incisive correspondence on a regular basis with the *Goleuad*, and more occasionally with the *Cymro*.

By his tenth birthday, Tudor had missed more schooling at Whitchurch Primary than he attended, due to a weak chest that has continued to be a lifelong complaint. Taking pity on him his teacher, Miss Mordecai, would always save the blackcurrant sweets for him from the box of Rowntree's Fruit Gums when she brought the class a treat. "It's to do him good," she would say. School attendance wasn't helped by the added distraction of being taken out of school early on the days when he did attend. A retired Methodist minister used to volunteer to walk Tudor to school, but after a time sitting in the park opposite, the old man soon got bored and took his young charge home, long before the end of the school day.

Certain dates etch themselves on the mind, more recently 9/11 and 7/7, from school history lessons 1066 and 1666, but for today's older generation September 3rd 1939 stands out as the day when Britain declared war on Germany. For the congregation of the Tabernacle, Whitchurch, however, it marked the commencement of a new ministry that Sunday morning. Against the background of national uncertainty and emergency Rev. Rheinallt Nantlais Williams climbed the pulpit steps to deliver his first sermon to his new congregation. Although the war years left the church without its minister when he enrolled as an Army Chaplain, for Tudor the coming of Rheinallt to Whitchurch would be the beginning of a lifelong influence. This is obvious when one hears him prefix a remark still with the words "as my minister used to say", and nobody doubts which minister he is referring to. Neither could have foreseen a day some twelve years later when that ten-year old boy would sit at the feet of his former minister, now Professor at the United Theological College, Aberystwyth. By this time also his friend from school and chapel, Megan Evans, had become Mrs. Rheinallt Nantlais Williams thus further cementing a happy friendship between both families.

For Tudor, there were still six years of schooling at Whitchurch Secondary to go through, career choices to consider, and a first degree to be taken at University College, Cardiff. People who know him often say that he could have been a doctor, a lawyer or a minister. Certainly, his skill in debate, prosecuting or defending an issue to its conclusion would suggest that he could have taken up law, but he himself says that he never considered it. His interest in herbal cures and traditional medicine, along with his experience of ill health did make him consider being a *missionary* doctor. But as a schoolboy he set his mind on the Queen of the Sciences, and so he followed his calling into theology and the ministry.

It was as a young teenager that he heard the evangelist, Dr. Stephen Olford speaking in a convention, and in those moments formally yielded his life to Christ. However he attributes many other influences at home, in the Tabernacle, and in para-church organizations as contributory factors in his conversion as well as that one meeting. Typically of Tudor, when he heard that the evangelist was later retelling his testimony, he was quite put out that the facts didn't quite match what he felt had been the case. He has always firmly believed that illustrations and testimonies should never be embellished for effect.

The Christian life is one of growth, interspersed with fresh outpourings of the Holy Spirit. One particularly blessed experience was as a Glamorgan Presbytery East's student representative at the Barry Missionary Conference. As a result he wrote out two hymns that summarised his response to God during those few days – "Breathe on me breath of God" and "O Jesus, I have promised". A second visit to the same Conference in 1957 was the means of his hearing a missionary nurse, Miss May Bounds, speak of the need for medical staff in Durtlang Hospital. This inspired him to raise support for the education of a young Indian doctor amongst the churches at Burry Green, Old Walls, and Cheriton. Although Dr. Biakmawia has long since graduated and made an impact as a surgeon in North-east India before retiring himself, concern for the progress of the Gospel and the practical needs of the Third World remains a priority for the members of the Pastorate.

His mother and father made their home, *Maes Cynlais*, a true Bethany to visiting ministers, missionaries, schoolboys and under-graduates. The Rev. Derek Swann recalls the night before an impor-tant Hebrew examination sitting in Tudor's home, Mrs. Lloyd supplying the food, while Tudor coached his young friend long into the night. It was all in a good cause, and had its desired effect. Derek passed, going on to become a Congregational Minister at Pontnewydd near Cwmbran, but not before he had invited Tudor to be best man at his wedding.

In his undergraduate years in Cardiff, firm friendships were formed that remain still. Similarly, local ministers like the Rev. Glyn Owen (Heath), Rev. Jack Sharman (Saltmead) and Dr. Gwyn Walters (Memorial Hall) proved to be a paradigm of Christian ministry. Dr. Arnold Aldis and Bill Capper of Newport were amongst the Christian Union speakers who made a lasting impression.

While he is interested in Gospel work wherever it is taking place, the traditional mission field of the Presbyterian Church of Wales has a special place in his heart. His mother, as a girl, collected pennies and subscriptions to help those serving in north-east India. Home visits by missionaries from the Khasi Hills enthralled him as a child. The names

Welsh IVF Conference at Borth, July, 1951. Seated in the front row from left to right are Gilmour Davies, Pegi Sharman, Megan Williams, Bethan Lloyd-Jones, D. Martyn Lloyd-Jones, Rhenallt N. Williams, Jack Sharman, Gwyn Walters, and Wynford Davies. Tudor Lloyd is at the extreme right of the fourth row from the front, standing next to the pillar.

of missionaries like Dr. Gordon Roberts, Dr. Arthur Hughes, and the Rev. Sidney Evans, together with place names like Aizawl, Shillong and Durtlang were part of the household vocabulary. At times he has denied himself a holiday or other luxury so that the money saved could be used in one of the mission hospitals, or for some other charitable cause. It disappoints him when he occasionally sees organisations spending too liberally what benefactors have struggled to give. In 1994, he went at his own expense to visit the Church in Mizoram when they were celebrating 100 years of Christian life amongst their people. He found it a moving experience to meet some people whose fathers had been headhunters within living memory, as well as the first couple to be married in a Christian ceremony. Out of their sense of debt to the Welsh Calvinistic Methodist Church, they entertained Tudor like a bishop.

Studying for his first degree provided Tudor with a fluency in Hebrew that still stands him in good stead. So when it was time to enter the Theological College at Aberystwyth he was well equipped to tackle the University of Wales B.D. Although he enjoyed renewing links with his old minister, Professor R. Nantlais Williams, he found the uncompromisingly critical and modernist stance towards the Scriptures of others on the staff especially unbearable. Ideas such as the *Graf Wellhausen* hypothesis *(JEDP)* that in 1952 were being superseded by other theories, were propounded as the only way to understand the Pentateuch, and other parts of the Old Testament. So in 1954 he transferred to Westminster College, Cambridge where he enrolled for Part 3 of the *Theological tripos*. Attending lectures by some of the great scholars of the time like C. F. D. Moule, John A. T. Robinson, Gordon Rupp, and H. H. Farmer helped him develop his powers of logic and thought. Graduating in 1956, he became in time a Master of Arts of the University of Cambridge.

These were the early days of Tyndale House, the now world-class Biblical Research Library where Rev. Derek Kidner was to become Warden. He has continued his association with the House through the years, and before retiring he spent sabbatical and holiday study time there. It was in the course of one of these later visits that Tudor

Staff and Students, United Theological College, Aberystwyth, 1953-54. The gowned teaching staff from left to right were: Rheinallt N. Williams, Basil Hall, W. R. Williams (Principal), Hedley Perry, and Ivor Enoch. Tudor Lloyd is behind Rheinallt Williams; this book's Editor is at the extreme right of the same row.

pursued an inaccuracy in the *Good News Bible* translation of a verse in Psalm 110: 1, 'The LORD said unto my Lord' an exact translation of the Hebrew. However, the translators had added to this phrase the words, 'the King'. Tudor insisted that our Lord's argument rested solely on the Hebrew. That version's error was being copied, as in the Mizo Bible, a further cause for concern. The validity of Tudor's point was recognized by at least one expert, Père Jacques Tournay, the former Director of l'Ecole Biblique. With that dogged determination so typical of him, Tudor pestered the Bible Society until they amended their text in its future editions.

On one of his visits he arranged that the Bursar of Tyndale House should fill the pulpit in the Gower Pastorate during his absence. This is how the Rev. Iain B. Hodgins was introduced to the churches that eventually invited him to be his successor in 1995.

Having satisfied the Candidates Board of the Presbyterian Church of Wales that he had fulfilled the requirements for ordination, Tudor's thoughts began turning to his future place of service. He decided in his mind that he would go to the first place that invited him to be their minister.

The Rev. Medford W. T. Lloyd had not long left Old Walls, Burry Green and Cheriton to serve a larger congregation at Beech-wood Park, Newport. Naturally, he was keen to see the vacancy he had created filled because as Medford put it "they waited years before I was appointed", and he had no wish to see the progress he had made in six years suffer. According to Rev. David Williams (Port Talbot) approaches had been made to thirteen other ministers about the pastorate before it was suggested that an approach be made to Mr. B. Tudor Lloyd. This was done, and one August Saturday evening, Tudor arrived in Burry Green in readiness to take services the next day. First impressions are not always the best, and despite his earlier resolve to accept the first offer from a church, upon alighting from the bus he secretly hoped his future would not be in rural Gower! Maybe having lived in towns and cities he found Burry Green unfamiliar territory, quite unlike what he was used to. People he met in that initial twenty-four hours were so kind, hospitable and welcoming that when eventually a call was extended, he accepted it without delay. So on All Saints Day 1956, a new minister for Burry Green, Cheriton, Llangennith and Old Walls again occupied the Manse.

When Rev. T. J. Lewis tried to encourage Rev. Medford Lloyd to move to Newport, he had implied to his young friend that if he didn't get out of Burry Green soon, he would vegetate there. The long and scholarly pastorate of his successor has totally disproved that notion. Instead, Tudor has used his base in Burry Green to read, write, prepare sermons and pray. In 1960 he completed the B. D. (Wales) degree that he had left unfinished when he moved to Cambridge. Gareth and Philip John, members of Old Walls recall how they would come upon Tudor walking the lanes and narrow roads of Gower reading his Greek New Testament at the same time. What they didn't realise is that he had bought the late Rev. John Viner's New Testament, carefully removed each book and placed each part between cardboard covers so that he could refer to Greek and English as he traversed the roads of Gower. Thirty years later when Apple computers were virtually unheard of outside university circles, Tudor purchased his first Apple Mac computer, as a revolutionary tool for his Biblical studies.

His induction took place in Old Walls on 3rd November 1956, as he had been ordained a month earlier in Rhostyllen on 3rd October. Not surprisingly, his mentor Professor R. Nantlais Williams, M.B.E., M.A. delivered the Charge to the Minister, whilst another influential figure Rev. D. O. Calvin Thomas, M.A. (Trinity, Wrexham) gave the Charge to the Church. These two ministers were influential in beginning the Youth Holiday Fellowship at Aberystwyth in the early 1950s. Significant numbers of the Church's young people from all over Wales attended, and were blessed or converted. Many who are now elders and mainstays in churches today met Tudor in that period. He values these acquaintances still. YHF proved to be a unifying force amongst the English churches of the Connexion, and throughout the next twenty years produced a steady flow of candidates for the ministry.

As a young minister, he made the occasional *faux pas*. Like the time he wore a sports jacket to a Presbytery meeting. Later, he discovered that he had been *blackballed* when his name had been suggested as the preacher for some special meetings in Trinity Presbyterian Church, Clydach. Dr. Stan Townsend the formidable Secretary of that church declared that someone who wore a sports jacket to Presbytery wasn't suitable to preach at his church! Another time, at the close of the year he decided to inform the locals of Burry Green that New Year had dawned by ringing a bell at midnight. Next day some irate residents were talking about the *clown* who had gone around ringing a bell in the middle of the night. Whatever misjudgments he may have made, people in Gower invariably speak about him with warm affection, and hold him in the highest regard.

Outside his pastorate, when he has antagonised colleagues in the courts of the Church he has done so in a way that has won their regard, despite the fact that they violently disagree with his views. His stance on the World Council of Churches, Cytun and the catch-all Connexional Contribution with its compulsory levies towards ecumenical activities, are well known. The W.C.C. Special Fund was a particular concern that he investigated, compelling the Church to cease supporting it. He discovered that those funds were being used to fund insurgents like Robert Mugabe in Africa. On another occasion in 1990 after the present *Book of Services* was published by the Panel of Doctrine, he was appalled to see the inclusion of readings from the Apocrypha as though they were Scripture, as well as prayers for the dead. Hopefully in 2007, a new book will be released that will be more in keeping with the Reformed teaching of the Church. At times he has stood alone, but when he has opposed someone publicly, they have been surprised to receive a letter within a few days to reassure them of his friendship despite their different viewpoint.

He is well versed in the procedure for conducting business and church meetings. If he sees that rules and order are being flouted, he is not slow to call for order. On one occasion in an Association Meeting when discussion on a certain issue was not allowed, he uttered the words *sieg heil* from his seat as he felt that the Moderator was flouting his authority. Those were unhappy days in the Connexion when a sizeable number of evangelical ministers and members seceded over ecumenicity and the Church's refusal to honour the 1823 Confession of

Faith. Whilst these issues are dealt with in a later chapter, the blind adherence to ecumenical dogma and the dream of Church Union by the majority left those who remained within the denomination isolated and looked upon with suspicion. Sadly, those outside the Presbyterian Church, who had previously preserved fellowship on evangelical and reformed convictions, now banded together as an exclusive fraternity on the additional basis of no involvement in a doctrinally mixed denomination. Within Presbyterianism, twenty-five years would pass before Tudor became accepted enough to be elected Moderator of the Association in 1998. Today, many of the issues that he once contended for as an almost lone voice have found a resonance with others of a rising generation.

Correspondence has been a treasured aspect of his pastoral care throughout the years. His thoughtfulness in putting pen to paper to empathise with neighbours, as well as members in times of illness and bereavement has endeared him to many. In a similar way the house-bound received post cards from his holidays when he was away from home.

Although his sermons are carefully prepared using the Scriptures in their original languages, he has not been widely known as a preacher beyond Swansea and Gower. However, Bible loving Christians of all denominations have appreciated his ministry and fellowship while on holiday in the locality. In days when there were fewer evangelical ministers, his ministry was known as one where newcomers could find food for their souls in the area. Those who find long sermons irksome never do so when Mr. Lloyd is the preacher. Sometimes, his hearers feel that he finishes his messages far too quickly out of a concern for not wearying the congregation. Quotations from notable preachers come from a variety of sources, from Calvin, Luther and Spurgeon as well as from the giants of the Welsh pulpit. Unlike some preachers, he does not confine his views or thoughts to be seen to be in tune with any particular theologian, preacher or branch of Reformed thought. For all that, he has been invited through the years to deliver the statutory sermons to the wider Church in the Association. Most notable is his Revival Memorial Lecture (2002) that is included in this volume.

The mid-week prayer meeting and Bible Study has been an important feature of church life during his time in the churches. He has tried to encourage individuals to pray briefly at the meetings. For him the spiritual side of church life has been more important than social activities. During his period, emphasis was deflected from fund raising activities to stewardship and free-will offerings as a means of supporting the churches. Like Hudson Taylor, his maxim is 'God's work done in God's way will never lack God's support'.

He has a close affinity with God's ancient people, the Jews. He feels deeply not just for those who were persecuted during the Nazi era, but whenever he sees or reads anything that belittles Jewry. He has paid homage with tears, along with his friend, Mr Ion Thomas (Pontarddulais) at Yad Vashem, the Holocaust Memorial in Jerusalem. A photograph taken in the Ffynnone Synagogue, Swansea records the occasion when he presented the Chief Rabbi with a wall clock. Although it is inscribed in Welsh with the words, "the God of Jacob is our refuge", he read the verse in Hebrew at the time.

In retirement he has accepted invitations to preach to the numerous Welsh-speaking churches around Neath and the Swansea Valley. Very often after struggling to compose a sermon in Welsh, he has overheard people muttering on the way out that they wished he had delivered it in English – not because his Welsh is poor, but because their own understanding of the language is so limited!

In the early 1990's he began turning his thoughts to the future when his tenure in Gower would be over. Initially, he wondered about sharing the work with an associate minister, which was a novel idea within the Presbyterian Church of Wales at the time. In his selfless way, he envisaged sharing his stipend with a colleague, dividing the work in the five churches. Although some discussions took place along these lines, the idea was eventually dropped. Instead he decided to retire early after 38 years service. Although there was no need for him to do so, he felt his health prevented him doing all he would like to accomplish in the pastorate.

In November 2006 Tudor Lloyd will have resided at the Manse in Burry Green for fifty years. As *Minister Emeritus*, he continues to assist by preaching in the churches of the pastorate, being quietly supportive in their activities and offering advice when it is sought. Unlike many retired ministers, he has been determined to find his niche in the background, thereby allowing his successor freedom to develop his ministry and to lead the churches.

By now his name is synonymous with the area. Just as people talk of Matthews (Ewenni), David Jones (Llangan) or Phillip Jones (Porthcawl), today the Rev. B Tudor Lloyd is rightly known as Tudor Lloyd (Gower).

2. 'This heap is a witness'

David Boorman

When Protestantism began to replace the Roman Catholic Church in Wales, many regarded it as 'ffydd y Saeson', the faith of the English, a foreign imposition. While at Haverfordwest, William Barlow as early as 1534 complained about resistance to reform, and during his time as Bishop of St. David's, 1536-1542, was in constant conflict with other clerics over matters of faith and discipline. This was bad enough, but worse was to follow.

Robert Ferrar, who was consecrated bishop in 1548 at a service in English, rather than Latin, was also opposed by them. When Mary came to the throne, his uncompromising Protestantism brought not only censure but also martyrdom. He met his death by being burned at the stake in Carmarthen market square on 30 March 1555. Another fervent Protestant, Richard Davies, bishop of St. David's 1561-1581, argued that Protestantism was nothing other than New Testament Christianity, torn from the Celtic Church by Rome, and now restored. A dearth of Gospel preaching in Wales at this time was drawn to the attention of Parliament in 1587 on behalf of John Penry. His zeal for reform issued in the publication of a series of tracts, in which he attacked not only Roman errors but also Episcopal neglect. The ecclesiastical settlement under Elizabeth I leant heavily on the support of bishops, so that in 1593 Penry, at the age of 30, was executed for what was reckoned to be treason. With the publication in 1588 of a Welsh Bible, and the Puritan thrust for urgency in preaching and purity of worship in the next century, reform was spreading in Wales.

However, it was not until after the execution of Charles I in January 1649 that the Puritans could attempt to carry through a programme of thorough reformation. There was particular concern for what were described as "the dark corners of the land". Wales was considered to be one such corner and all its constituent counties were branded as abounding "in ignorance and profaneness". In 1650 Parlia-

The martyrdom of Robert Ferrar, Carmarthen, 1555.
This plaque to his memory is in Nott Square.

ment sought to tackle the problem by means of an "Act for the better Propagation and Preaching of the Gospel in Wales". This has been described as "a deliberate attempt to puritanize Wales". Commissioners appointed under the Act examined and ejected incumbents of livings for delinquency and malignancy (in other words, for clinging to Anglican practices) and for non-residence.

Even during the years immediately before the outbreak of, and during, the Civil War, there had been a number of individual and official initiatives in seeking to bring the Gospel to Swansea and Gower. Four men in particular are associated with the establishment and spread of evangelical nonconformity and, more importantly, of Gospel truth in Swansea and in Gower from the 1640s onwards – Marmaduke Matthews, Ambrose Mostyn, John Miles, and Daniel Higgs. As early as 1636 Matthews, (a native of Llangyfelach), installed in the living of Penmaen, was in trouble with the Bishop of Saint David's, who reported him as preaching "against the keeping of all holy days with divers others, as fond, or profane opinions". Threatened with pro-ceedings in the Court of High Commission, he migrated to New England in 1638. Matthews's experiences in New England, where he held pastorates at Yarmouth and Malden, were not altogether happy. On one occasion the religious authorities fined him £10 for preaching in an "unauthorised" congregation and then called him to answer the charge, brought by a member of his own congregation, of "preaching divers unsound, erroneous and unsafe opinions". It must have been with some relief that he returned to Wales in 1654 at the request of Colonel Philip Jones to become vicar of St John's, Swansea.

Ambrose Mostyn, who "had a genius for unravelling difficult texts and abhorred unpremeditated sermons", was appointed "lecturer" at Pennard by the Long Parliament in 1642 at the request of the parishioners. As a lecturer, supported financially by the parishioners, Mostyn was expected to preach each Sunday morning and afternoon without any obstacles being placed in his way by the vicar. It is not clear for how long Mostyn continued to hold this position. What is certain is that, within a few years, he was receiving £50 a year from the Committee for Plundered Ministers (possibly to augment other sources of income) in return for which he was "required to preach and officiate as well in the parish church of Swansea as in the parishes and places thereto adjacent". Mostyn was responsible for the formation of the first "gathered" church in Swansea (that is, a church which com-prises only those who have freely responded to the Gospel and voluntarily accepted the responsibilities of membership). From the late 1640s onwards Mostyn was active in preaching the Gospel in North Wales.

If of no greater value and importance than the labours of such men as Mostyn and Matthews, better known is the work of John Miles, centred on the Calvinistic Baptist church at Ilston. Miles settled at Ilston as the result of an initiative taken in 1649 by the Particular Baptist congregation meeting at Glaziers' Hall in Broad Street, London. In that year John Miles and his friend Thomas Proud, both of whom had recently come to Baptist convictions, arrived in London from Glamorgan and met with the Glaziers' Hall Baptists. The latter had been praying for evangelists to preach "in those places where the Lord had work to be done". Miles and Proud seemed to be God's answer to the church's prayers; following their baptism, they were, as the Ilston Churchbook records, "again recommended into these parts". Why they should have made their way to a remote parish in Gower is not clear although it has been suggested that Miles had served in the Parliamentary army in the locality.

Whatever the reason, their mission soon began to bear fruit for "after a fortnight's time or thereabouts, it pleased the Lord to give some earnests of his design to gather a people to himself to walk in communion with these his servants". The first converts were two women, baptised in October 1649, to be followed by another four women before any men were added to the fellowship. By October 1650 the Ilston Baptists numbered 43 and by the end of that year Miles had baptized his fiftieth member. The last baptism recorded in the Churchbook occurred in August 1660, a few months after the return of Charles II. By then, the Ilston Baptist church had a little over 250 members.

Little is known about Miles's early years. He was born in 1621 in a Welsh-speaking part of Herefordshire and matriculated at Brasenose College, Oxford in 1636. It was only from 1649 onwards that he became a significant figure in the history of evangelical noncon-formity. At Ilston he served as rector of the parish church in place of an ejected royalist, William Houghton. From 1649 until 1660 the Ilston Baptists met in the parish church of St. Illtyd though they always referred to the place as their 'Meeting House', not their 'church' or 'chapel'. Baptist services and meetings were open only to members. Indeed, Miles was insistent that non-baptized sympathisers should not be allowed to attend. But Miles would also have held more general services for all the parishioners of Ilston, the majority of whom remained non-Baptists.

The members of the Ilston congregation were drawn not only from villages and hamlets all over Gower but also from the east of Swansea and north of the Loughor estuary. The four women who, with John Miles and Thomas Proud, constituted the church at its inception came from Llanddewi, Paviland, Ilston and "Kevengorwydd" (possibly Cefngorwydd in the parish of Loughor). Before long members were being added from such places as Baglan, Margam, Aberavon, Briton Ferry, Llanelli and Swansea. In an area where roads and transport were poor, this widely scattered membership inevitably created difficulties. As early as October 1650, and even before the church began to draw members from the east of Swansea, it was decided that the whole Baptist congregation should gather at Ilston "once in three weeks . . . upon the first day of the week to break bread together". On the other Sundays, and also on set weekdays, the congregation would divide and meet as a number of more local 'house-groups', in the houses of its leading members. Initially, there were three such groups, one meeting at Ilston, a second at Llanddewi for "our brothers and sisters in the west parts of Gower", and a third for those living in Carmarthenshire and "other Welsh parts" at the house of "sister Jennet Jones" in "Burwick" (possibly the hamlet of Berwick which forms part of the parish of Llanelli). But all serious matters, such as the baptism and admission of new members, advice to existing members who were planning to marry, and questions of discipline – during the 1650s a handful of members were expelled for drunkenness and sexual misconduct – were to be referred to the full Ilston meeting. There, too, training sessions on preaching took place and approval was given to new preachers. Although Miles had acted as leader of the church from its foundation, not until November 1651 did the Ilston Baptists formally appoint him as their pastor.

Miles was determined to spread the word throughout South Wales. In the early 1650s, and under his influence, further Baptist churches were founded elsewhere – at Hay on Wye and Llanharan/Llantrisant in 1650, at Carmarthen in 1651 and at Abergavenny in 1652. Sadly, the records of these churches are much poorer than those of the Ilston church. The five churches maintained close and regular contact and representatives from each met periodically to discuss points of difficulty or dispute and to maintain overall discipline. Between 1650 and 1656 at least seven such 'General Meetings' are known to have been held, the first at Ilston on 6 and 7 November, 1650.

Miles's star was in the ascendant during the 1650s. As well as his work with the Baptist churches, he was minister of Ilston parish, appointed an 'Approver' under the Act for the Propagation of the Gospel in Wales of February 1650 and named a 'Trier' under Oliver Cromwell's Church Ordinance of August 1654. As an "Approver" and, subsequently, a "Trier", Miles was one of a number of ministers (including Mostyn and three famous Welsh puritans, Walter Cradock, Vavasor Powell and Morgan Llwyd), responsible for licensing "godly and painful [that is, painstaking] men, of able gifts and knowledge for the work of the ministry, and of approved conversation for piety", to preach the Gospel in Wales.

The Ilston Church Book lists the names of 261 men and women who were added to the church from its foundation in the autumn of 1649 until the summer of 1660, the year which saw the restoration of the monarchy in the person of Charles II. Reflecting on "some principal providences of our Father towards us, his poor despised people", the church placed on record the fact that "we cannot choose but admire at the unsearchable wisdom, power, and love of God in bringing about his own designs far above and beyond the capacity and understanding of the wisest of men. Thus, to the glory of his own great name, hath he dealt with us, for when there had been no companies or society of people holding forth and practising the doctrine, worship, order, and discipline of the Gospel according to primitive institution that ever we heard of in all Wales since the apostasy, it pleased the Lord to choose this dark corner to place his name here . . ." What, in their eyes, made the Ilston church distinctive was the fact that they were the first church in Wales to practise "the glorious ordinance of baptism".

Daniel Higgs was a Worcester man, educated at Oxford, who during the Commonwealth period exercised an itinerant ministry in Carmarthenshire and Glamorganshire under the terms of the 1650 Act for the Better Propagation of the Gospel in Wales. Within three years, he was settled at Rhosili. Although Higgs, a popular Independent preacher, only held the living until 1661, his short ministry had a profound impact on the spiritual life of the parish. For the next three hundred years nonconformity remained strongly entrenched in village life.

Although they were nonconformists, Miles, Matthews and Higgs, and others like them, replaced Anglican ministers who were ejected from their livings. William Houghton was ejected from Ilston, Hopkin Morgan from Swansea, and Edward Gamage from Rhosili. The last of these took up farming! Among other men who were forced to leave was Hugh Gore of Oxwich. After the Restoration Gore became a bishop in Ireland but he is remembered principally as the founder of Swansea Grammar School.

For better or worse, the "reign" of the nonconformists effectively came to an end following the restoration of the monarchy in May 1660. The degree to which nonconformists would suffer was not apparent immediately. Before his return to his kingdom Charles II had promised to grant "a Liberty to tender Consciences", and Presbyterians, at least, were hopeful that there would be a settlement embracing both them and Anglicans. Among the hopefuls was Daniel Higgs who was presented to the living of Port Eynon by the King in August 1660. Before long, however, these hopes were to be proved vain – partly because there was a widespread desire among the population as a whole for the restoration of the Church of England and especially because Charles's first parliament, known as the Cavalier Parliament, was in no mood for compromise. By 1661 some Anglican ministers who had been ejected under the Commonwealth were repossessing their former livings, among them Edward Gamage at Rhosili. Although Higgs's ministry had profoundly affected some, it had angered others; it was alleged that, when he was expelled from Rhosili, he was "forced to leave his wife and seven children for fury of the mob".

Trouble followed trouble for nonconformist ministers and their flocks as the Cavalier Parliament enacted one measure after another in an attempt to suppress nonconformity. Following the passing, in 1662, of the Act of Uniformity which required ministers to conform to the liturgy of the Church of England, as prescribed in the Book of Common Prayer, about 2,000 clergy were forced to give up their livings. Of 23 men ejected from their livings in Glamorgan between 1660 and 1662, seven were from Gower: Evan Griffith (Oxwich), Daniel Higgs (Rhosili), James Jones (Llangyfelach), Morgan Jones (Llanmadoc), Marmaduke Matthews (Swansea), John Miles (Ilston), and Thomas Proud (Cheriton).

Two Conventicle Acts, one of 1664 and another of 1670, threatened people who attended, or preached at, or made their homes available for nonconformist meetings, with fines, imprisonment, and even transportation. The Five Mile Act of 1665 forbade ejected ministers from residing within five miles of their old parish or any corporate town.

How, then, did the nonconformists in Gower fare when confronted with such punitive legislation? What courses of action were open to them? One possibility was to do what some of their nonconformist forefathers had done under the earlier Stuart monarchs – that is, to emigrate to the New World. This path was eventually to be followed by John Miles and some of the Ilston congregation. However, there is a strong local tradition (but with no contemporary documentary evidence) that, for a time, Miles and his congregation made use of a small, rectangular chapel, known as Trinity Well chapel, dating from the Middle Ages, and situated about half a mile southwest of the parish church of Ilston. Whether this was the case or not, the fact remains that, at some point between 1663 and 1666, Miles and his followers sailed for North America where they founded the town, and first church, of Swansea, Massachusetts.

Another possibility was to lie low, meet (as far as possible) in secret, and hope for better days. Such action was certainly taken in various places in England and in south-west Scotland and may possibly have occurred in Wales. There certainly were "conventicles" provid-

Ruins of Trinity Well Chapel, Ilston. Miles and his congregation may have worshipped here after the Restoration of Charles II.

The memorial tablet at Ilston.

ing ministry and fellowship for Swansea and Gower nonconformists during the 1660s. Although Ilston was no longer the centre for the Calvinistic Baptists after the departure of Miles for America, Miles's mantle fell on the shoulders of Lewis Thomas of Kenfig. Thomas was one among a number of men who had been charged by Miles in the 1650s with the responsibility of providing regular ministry for Ilston members living in the Neath and Swansea areas. In his *Wales under the Penal Code*, Thomas Richards pays tribute to Thomas in the following fulsome terms: "His record from the day he was made member of Ilston on 27 November, 1650, to the day he was licensed in 1672 at his new house in Swansea and up to the general supervision of Baptist causes, ranging from Blaenau Gwent in the east to Rhydwilym in the west, which only ceased with his death in 1704, proved that the old leader's mantle had fallen not unworthily on the shoulders of a man who preferred the dreary pathway of conventicles to place and power in Massachusetts".

What of Matthews and Higgs? There is something of a mystery here for, although Swansea was a corporate town and, as such, subject to the terms of the Five Mile Act, a number of ejected ministers seem to have settled and possibly exercised ministry there without being subjected to the full force of the law. A possible explanation is that local magistrates were sympathetic to the nonconformist cause. Marmaduke Matthews remained there throughout the 1660s and at some point Daniel Higgs moved to the town from Port Eynon. Another influential nonconformist minister, Stephen Hughes, moved there from Carmarthenshire. Nonconformist hopes were raised when Charles issued a Declaration of Indulgence in 1672, extending religious liberty to Protestant nonconformists on the one hand and Roman Catholics on the other, by suspending the execution of the penal laws that punished recusants from the Church of England. Under the terms of the Indulgence nonconformists could be licensed to preach or to have preaching in their houses. Higgs succeeded in obtaining licences for Swansea (at his own house), Bishopston (at the house of Henry Griffith), Nicholaston (at the house of Robert Gethin) and Rhosili (at the house of Richard Bevan), and Hughes obtained one for Swansea. The very first licence obtained for Wales was that granted to Marmaduke Matthews to preach at his own house in the Swansea parish of St John's. Lewis Thomas was licensed to preach in Swansea at the house of William Dykes.

Within three years the Indulgence was dead. It had aroused the anger of Parliament and of the Anglican episcopate. In 1675 Gilbert Sheldon, Archbishop of Canterbury, was able to persuade the king's Council to revoke the licences and to declare them invalid. Nonconformists would have to wait another fourteen years to gain their freedom. This was effected by the Toleration Act of 1689, by which time William and Mary had come to the throne, which ushered in better days for them. However, there is good reason to believe that the labours of men such as Miles, Thomas, Higgs, Matthews and Hughes had not been in vain and that there were men and women in Swansea and throughout Gower who had embraced the Gospel.

Seed had been sown; the harvest would come with the great eighteenth century revival of religion. If the Pastorate's spiritual heritage at that time appeared to be a mere 'heap of stones', they gave clear Gospel witness to the worship of God (Genesis 31: 44-48).

3. 'To set up the house of our God'

Eifion Evans

Turmoil and confusion in society and religion characterized the eighteenth century. In place of 'the City of God', by establishing Christ's kingdom, preaching Christ's cross, and building up Christ's people, men sought 'the City of Man'. It was a time when the accepted foundations were shaken, divine revelation was challenged by human reason, divine intervention was replaced by natural process, and heaven on earth was to be achieved by human effort. Thoughts of God were side-lined since creation seemed to sustain itself, and human potential seemed unbounded. An 'information explosion' took place, with the appearance of a new kind of book, the encyclopaedia. This demonstrated immense diversity in the world, all of it accessible to the human mind. The affirmation of human rights played down moral absolutes and talk about accountability before God receded into the background. If all this is beginning to sound familiar, that is not surprising: there are many parallels to the state of society today.

As now, so then: a beleaguered few maintained a Gospel witness in Gower, so that in the eighteenth century it was not entirely a spiritual wilderness. In the opinion of Glanmor Williams, Swansea became "the most lively centre of Dissent in Wales, having something of the order of 300-400 Nonconformists, and maybe more, in the borough and its environs." Against the rising barrage of unbelief their weapons were preaching and teaching. They were fond of using a pulpit to evangelize, and a catechism to instruct, tools available to each new generation of labourers raised by God. The old Dissenting churches had survived a sterile period in the early eighteenth century. Some of their leaders, such as the Baptist Enoch Francis in Carmarthenshire, Philip Pugh the Cardiganshire Independent, and Edmund Jones the Independent 'old prophet' of Monmouthshire, by their faithful labours gave evidence of a hidden strength.

In the Swansea area Congregational churches did not come into their full strength until the century's end, with the coming of David Davies to Mynydd-bach. Born at Llangeler, Carmarthenshire in 1763, with little education, but after coming to faith in Christ, a man with Methodist-like passion for preaching and for souls, his early ministry was on the Cardiganshire–Carmarthenshire border. His ministry at Mynydd-bach bore much fruit, and in 1803 he built Ebenezer chapel in Swansea, from 1808 labouring here and at Sketty. Tudur Jones reckoned that he was the most dynamic of Congregational preachers, while R. T. Jenkins spoke of him as "an exceptionally powerful preacher . . . a planter of churches and trainer of preachers." Another historian, John Thomas, reckoned that "he was one of the most gifted preachers, with a voice like a silver bell, so that the hardest men could hardly bear his ministry without melting under it . . . He transformed the entire tenor of his denomination's ministry. He broke down its sterile, monotonous manner, and introduced elements of fervour and life." One preacher speaks of taking a three-week journey with Davies, with the latter preaching twice or three times a day, on each occasion the congregation staying behind in the building, weeping and praising. An Independent chapel at Crwys, Llanrhidian was built in 1788 and rebuilt in 1831. Its minister from 1819 was John Evans, whose charge also included Brynteg, near Loughor, and from 1839 he also undertook the oversight of the flock at Lady Barham's chapel in Penclawdd. He ministered, and taught at a school as well, until his death in January 1856.

The nineteenth century had to dawn before the area would also see the emergence of a vigorous Calvinistic Methodism. What, then of Gospel witness in the intervening years in Gower? This was promoted by members of the Anglican Church, often at odds with their ecclesiastical superiors on account of their evangelical convictions and zeal. Fired by God's reviving grace in their hearts, they sought 'to set up the house of our God' (Ezra 9:9) throughout the land, and Gower was not altogether neglected by their efforts.

It would have been with the help of sympathetic clergymen that Griffith Jones, Rector of Llanddowror from 1716 until his death in 1761, began organizing 'circulating charity schools' in Gower in 1740.

He did so from a conviction that 'Christianity is taught and not caught', using the Bible and his catechisms as textbooks. The schools, lasting for a period of three months, were intended for adults as well as children. They were usually held in the evening and avoided busy times in the farming calendar. In the period 1740-70 the lists of scholars show that several hundreds attended, with 120 at one school in Llanrhidian parish alone. While Jones's vision was primarily to educate people in Welsh, it also embraced the monoglot English in Wales. He was committed, as he confessed on one occasion, to "the conscientious and constant use of all the means of grace, to serve as buckets to fetch living waters from the wells of salvation."

Along with Jones's educational evangelism, God raised a fiery, preaching evangelist, Howel Harris of Trefeca, near Talgarth, in Breconshire. Another Anglican, he was converted in 1735, and such

was his passion for souls that he was unwilling to go to bed at night without having spoken to someone of Christ and of their need to trust in Him alone for salvation. Nor could his zeal find adequate expression in his own locality. Throughout his life he, too, remained a member of the Episcopal Church, even though he was refused ordination by the bishop. His visits to Gower started in May, 1742, and even though they were not numerous, he kept his finger on the Peninsula's spiritual pulse through the reports of others. From Rhosili he writes on 4th May: "The work of our dear Lord goes wondrously on everywhere. Prejudice falls. Societies are regulated and established, the weak strengthened. Love and liberty make way to many souls. In some places they come to hear by thousands." The next day he records a visit to Crwys, in Llanrhidian parish, where he "had great power". Writing from Swansea early in 1743 to the English clergyman and itinerating evangelist, George Whitefield, he has this to say: "Yesterday I discoursed just by this town to about two thousand; most were very serious, and many wept sore. I had a call to the town today. Some of the better sort heard and were somewhat affected. In the morning I discoursed at a burial, before the corpse was taken out; and heard one of the best sermons I ever heard as to sound doctrine, on, 'If any man be in Christ, he is a new creature', by a Church minister, Mr. John Price of Llangyfelach. I am called to another seaport town near here as soon as I can come, where I never was before." Further visits by Harris are recorded, in May 1745, October 1749, and January 1765, and at other times, he brushed the Gower boundary by visiting Loughor and Gorseinon.

Whitefield himself had preached at Swansea in April 1743, and some of Harris's comments on that occasion are interesting: "the Lord did favour us with His presence; indeed I am persuaded it was a happy day to many souls . . . He preached very sweet on Jacob's ladder; he now discoursed with such convincing arguments and attended with such power that I trust many were reached . . . I was indeed melted down, while admiring the amazing tenderness and condescension of God to poor worms, in giving gifts etc. to suit their taste in order to engage their attention and to win them to Christ, and to remove their prejudice." As a result a society, or fellowship meeting, was set up in the town, whose members desired similar preachers to visit them. Before the end of the century one of Whitefield's patrons, the Countess of Huntingdon, had opened one of her chapels in the town.

Early in 1745 one of Harris's fellow-labourers, John Richard of Llansamlet, wrote of a visit he and another layman had paid to the area. "I have been with my brother James Ingram, listening to him discoursing at Newton [near Mumbles], where many people heard him, and in truth I can say through experience that the Lord came there to meet us. Blessed, be His Name, Amen. I believe God blessed that meeting in opening certain hearts there to receive God's missionaries, if not God Himself. You would be surprised to know the tenderness that God showed towards their spirits. I fully believe that someone will be honoured by God to be an instrument in His hands to call many souls in their midst . . . I feel in my heart as the lion feels for its prey for retrieving those souls under the dominion of Satan, and I fully believe that some of them are Christ's sheep, and He must needs gather them." Richard regretted his inability to preach in English, and so prayed that God would "send them one near to His heart . . . and hasten the time." William Griffith, 'Apostle of Gower', of whom more later, may well have been the answer to his believing prayer.

Society reports for this area were written by Thomas William, and in 1747 he says of Newton, that "God has something to do here", but of Llwyn-onn, near Ilston, "It is alarmingly dead here." A little over a year later, conditions at Newton were "the same as before", but his remarks about Llwyn-onn are more extensive. "They come together here every Wednesday night. They are simple, [though] unbelieving souls. Thomas James of Loughor has had one of them in his congregation, who I think has previously been brought home [that is, to faith in Christ], perhaps through contact with some of the members in his society, and who seek to draw others, too, if possible. I don't know whether it is right to keep some of his society in our fellowship? Some of those who are members of Loughor Society know the Lord [and] have been allowed to remain, but from what I can gather, there is something lacking in them, for those who share fellowship with them are the ones ready to halt [that is, remain uncommitted]." Such Christian laymen faced many difficulties, and one of them refers to moving house "to the other side of Pen-clawdd, to a dark, pagan place." Like the biblical Ezra, they faced difficulties with the confidence that mercy had been extended to them 'to give us a reviving, to set up the house of our God' (9:9).

Oxwich cottage where John Wesley preached.

Another Methodist preacher, John Wesley, landed at Pen-clawdd in 1758, and preached on a rainy day in a barn at Newton "about six miles from Swansea . . . and it pleased God to send a gracious rain upon their hearts." In his *Journal* for that day, August 28th, Wesley adds a significant note: "After preaching at Swansea in the evening I met those who desired to join in a society, and explained to them the nature and design of it, with which they were quite unacquainted." He was back in Swansea in 1763, preaching "to one or two hundred people, many of whom seemed full of good desires", but acknowledged sadly "as there is no society, I expect no deep or lasting work." When he preached in Swansea in later years the numbers attending were more impressive. In 1764 he preached "to a little company" that was "all attention" at Oxwich, which he visited again in 1767, 1769 and 1771, and the standard edition of his *Journal* has photographs of John Clarke's cottage in which the meetings were held. However, it was not until Welsh Wesleyan Methodist preachers came to South Wales in 1805 that the denomination took hold, sometimes by defection from Calvinistic Methodist ranks. The latter differed from Wesley and his followers by their belief in and commitment to the understanding of God's grace as sovereign, free and permanent in man's salvation, a position they held in common with John Calvin and Saint Augustine. The Wesleyans, on the other hand, were convinced that Scripture taught free will, a universal atonement, present assurance of salvation, entire sanctification, and the conditional perseverance of believers in grace. However, they shared in common an insistence on the new birth, on the need for personal faith in Christ for salvation, and an emphasis on 'heart-experience' as well as 'head-knowledge' of Gospel truths. Their favourite, and distinctive, means to safeguard this personal, experimental religion was the society meeting.

Conversion to Christ was a life-changing experience that was to be monitored and nurtured. It affected the whole personality and every area of life: the understanding the will, the emotions and the conscience. Such societies therefore promoted an openness to every aspect of discipleship from its members, and aimed at their spiritual maturity. William Williams, Pantycelyn, the hymn-writer, was deemed to be a supremely skilled physician of souls, and his writings for the use of the societies, in particular, his *Experience Meeting* showed an extraordinary insight and sensitivity in dealing with religious experience. In his eagerness to foster such societies in his day, William Griffiths of Gower was a true Calvinistic Methodist, and an able disciple of Williams. William Williams also gave expression to praise and prayer in his hymns, and there were others, too, within the denomination who were gifted in the same way: David Jones of Caio; Morgan Rhys of Llanfynydd, and later, Ann Griffiths. Their hymns had depth as well as rhyme, vivid imagery as well as memorable lines. They enriched the worship of God's people as well as building them up individually in their understanding of the Faith.

A contemporary sketch of William Williams, Pantycelyn.

Between the labours of these early Methodist Fathers and the ministry of William Griffiths there emerged in Gower a Gospel work of similar conviction and evangelistic zeal. Diana Middleton, later Baroness Barham (1762-1823) was an evangelical patron, whose parents "were devout evangelicals, deeply committed to religious philanthropy and reform, and closely involved in the movement for the abolition of slavery." She therefore had early contact with evangelical influences, and "became an ardent and active supporter of Methodism". In 1780 she had married an unlikely suitor and wealthy but eccentric landowner, Gerard Noel Edwardes, by whom she had several children. However, upon the death of her father in 1813, Diana could draw on independent means, and she separated from her husband, eventually setting up house at Fairy Hill. As well as several schools, she established a kind of mini-denomination of six chapels in Gower: Bethesda, Burry Green (opening in 1814); Bethel, Pen-clawdd (1816); Trinity, Cheriton (1816); Paraclete, Newton (1818); Immanuel, Pilton Green (1821); and Mount Pisgah, Parkmill (1822).

From 1789 to 1796 the Countess of Huntingdon's Swansea chapel was supplied by clergymen and Calvinistic Methodist preachers. At this latter date, William Kemp, a student from the Countess's College at Cheshunt, was appointed minister. When Lady Barham came to South Wales, it was Kemp who impressed upon her the great spiritual need in Gower. He also formed a very close friendship with William Griffiths, who preached for him at Swansea on at least one occasion. Kemp preached in English at Association meetings for the Calvinistic Methodists, at Llangeitho in March 1816. Griffiths was in the congregation, and it is possible that some measure of interest in the spiritual needs in Gower was aroused on that occasion. His only comments, however, were that "this was a great sermon to those who understood it", making two points from the text, Psalm 87:5, "1. that the Church will prosper; and 2. that the Church will endure." At the Fishguard Association in October Lady Barham's request for someone to preach and teach at a school was by its Committee directed to Griffiths and caused him a sleepless night. Six years later Kemp preached again at an Association at Llangadog, By this time he had returned to Cheshunt as a tutor, and William Griffiths had started his trail-blazing ministry in Gower.

Griffiths's roots lay in this emerging Calvinistic Methodist denomination. His spiritual heritage drew heavily on the evangelical nature of its preaching, on the discipline of the society meeting, and on the ordered framework of its monthly meeting and quarterly Association. These moulded his personal experience as well as his ministerial education. By the time that Griffiths commenced his labours in Gower, the denomination's distinctive features had been clearly established. It had only recently emerged from Anglicanism, not so much because it renounced an episcopal framework, but because it desired freedom to spread the Gospel and to nurture and discipline its converts. The problem was not so much one of formal doctrine or organization, as of spiritual life and growth.

Initially, the Thirty-nine Articles of the Church of England were deemed to be an adequate, systematic expression of doctrinal beliefs. This was often stated in the Trust Deeds of the early chapel buildings, with a particular emphasis on those Articles which set out the Calvinist understanding of God's work in salvation. The 1823 *Confession of Faith* sought to state the denominations doctrinal convictions in a fresh and distinctive manner, while conforming to biblical and Protestant standards such as the Westminster Confession of Faith of the Puritan period. The Constitutional Deed of 1826 gave denominational status and legal safeguards to the Calvinistic Methodists, in keeping with their convictions and practice.

Foremost among the new denomination's distinctive teachings was the insistence on personal faith in Christ. Preaching was given priority, but it was a particular kind of preaching. It presupposed the sinfulness of human nature, aimed at the conscience, sought conversion, and emphasised godly living. Only the initiative of God's grace and mercy could produce such a change, a new birth, and the agency God used, preaching and teaching, required the power of the Holy Spirit to make it effective. The next distinctive presupposed submission to Christ within the context of loving, caring fellowship and support, and this the converts found in the society meeting. It was intended to be a true means of grace, with prayer, teaching, and worship, but always within the constraints of sharing one's dealings with God for mutual benefit.

From the time of Howel Harris, Calvinistic Methodism was missionary-minded, reflecting his passion to win souls for Christ. One of Thomas Charles's schoolmasters, John Davies (1772-1855), from Montgomeryshire, felt called to labour with the London Missionary Society and sailed for Tahiti in 1800, where he would remain without furlough until his death in 1855. While training with the same Society, a converted German Jew, Joseph Samuel Christian Frederick Frey, began work among the Jews in London. In 1809 he founded the first modern mission to Jews, and on the invitation of Thomas Charles, he visited churches in North Wales to gain support for Gospel work among the Jews. Surprisingly, he preached at the first Calvinistic Methodist ordination in South Wales, at Llandeilo, in 1811, taking Isaiah 53:10 as his text. Shortly afterwards, an anonymous Welsh pamphlet appeared with the title *Cyfarchiad Gostyngedig at Grist'nogion Cymru o bob Enw, oddi wrth Gymdeithas Llundain, yr hon a sefydlwyd i'r diben o ddwyn ymlaen Grist'nogaeth ymysg yr Iddewon, gan ddeisyf eu cynorthwy, yn ol eu gallu, i ddwyn yr amcan i ben* ('A Humble Petition to Christian of whatever Name in Wales, from the London Society established to promote Christianity among the Jews, for support, according to their means, to realize this aim'). As a result of a Church of Scotland initiative, some ministers visited the Holy Land in 1838, among them the godly Robert Murray McCheyne and the writer on prophecy, Alexander Keith. Following a fervent plea by the latter at an Association at Ruthin in 1845 that the Christian Church should pray and work for the conversion of Abraham's seed, John Mills, originally from Llanidloes, was supported by the denomination to work among the Jews in London from 1846 until 1859. In 1841 Thomas Jones, from Montgomeryshire, took the Gospel to north-east India, to the Khasi hills of Assam, a move which resulted in the creation of a vibrant Christian Church. Another pioneering missionary effort faced grave difficulties. This was the work in Brittany, France, commenced in 1842 by a Carmarthenshire man, James Williams (1812-1893), where he remained for over 25 years, and was followed by Jenkyn Jones. By 1904 there were five churches, five more preaching stations, 85 converts from Roman Catholicism, and together with adherents and children the total number of hearers amounted to some 700. The work was eventually taken over by the native French Protestant Church.

The emergence and consolidation of the Calvinistic Methodist denomination therefore took place while William Griffiths was entering on his work in Gower. This left its stamp, not only on his ministry, but also on the kind of religion that the people of his churches practised. It was a religion that had at its heart the grace of God, personally experienced, mutually shared and lovingly displayed in everyday life. In the words of George Whitefield, "Methodism is no more nor less than 'Faith working by Love'; a holy method of living and dying, to the glory of God."

4. 'Foundations strongly laid'

Eifion Evans

A Topographical Dictionary of Wales by Samuel Lewis in 1833 describes Llanrhidian parish as "consisting of a Higher and Lower division, which separately maintain their own poor, and containing 1445 inhabitants, of which number, 1033 are in the Higher, and 412 in the Lower, division." After noting that a fair was usually held on Palm Monday, and the manufacture of woollen cloth "upon a very confined scale, employing no more than from six to eight persons", it goes on to speak of the churches: "The church is dedicated to St. Illtyd. In the Higher division of the parish is a chapel of ease, in which divine service is performed once a month by the incumbent, who also solemnizes marriages, christenings, and burials at this chapel, which is four miles distant from the parish church. In this division also there are places of worship for Baptists, a congregation in the late Countess of Huntingdon's connexion, and Independents; and in the Lower division, another belonging to the Countess of Huntingdon's connexion. Sunday schools, connected with the established church and the several dissenting congregations, are supported by subscription."

It was to this area that William Griffiths came early in 1817 as an unordained, unmarried, Calvinistic Methodist preacher at the invitation of Lady Barham. The late arrival of Calvinistic Methodism to Gower is explained in part by the fact that its inhabitants in the main spoke English. As the denomination expanded into English-speaking areas it was felt that an English Conference should be created which would at least give the work a measure of cohesion. At one of the English Quarterly Associations, on January 7th 1852, William Griffiths preached a sermon on Matthew 18:7 under the title 'Impediments to the progress of Christianity'. An account of Griffiths's life and ministry by the Rev. B. Tudor Lloyd appears as Appendix 1. However, it will be useful at this point to introduce him and to highlight some of his personal and ministerial qualities.

Manuscript of Griffiths's Association sermon.

As a regular contributor of articles to the denominational monthly, *Y Drysorfa*, Griffiths was known throughout the denomination for his sound theology and godly counsel. A kind of review article, written in 1855, was an appreciation of a work by John Hughes, *Methodistiaeth Cymru*, and reflects his own commitment to Calvinistic Methodism. This was before the appearance of a third and final volume which included a short section on the denomination's churches in Gower, but Griffiths found the work timely and encouraging. "As we read the account of these early fathers, the first thing that strikes us is their strong self-denial, and their resolve to separate from the evil world in order to cleave to Christ and His cause through all the trials and hindrances that crossed their path. The next thing, is their intense desire to enjoy Gospel ordinances. Another characteristic was their zealous desire to convert the souls of their neighbours. We cannot but notice the manner in which their religion began – with their turning from sinful ways to embrace Christ and the Gospel." He was also a regular contributor to the more local monthly, *Y Cylchgrawn*, published in Swansea with a similar purpose, to feed minds and strengthen souls in a Calvinistic Methodist understanding of biblical truth. (See Appendix 2 for a list of his articles in these two periodicals).

Griffiths was highly esteemed as an all-round, consistent Christian. He was methodical and orderly in his habits, solemn and fluent in his preaching. His aim was faithfulness, even though until the later years of his ministry there was no great spiritual harvest. In 43 years he was unable to preach on only two Sabbaths, and in addition to engagements on the Lord's Day he regularly preached at various locations on weeknights. He reckoned that in all he had preached some 15,000 times by the end of his life. He also showed exceptional zeal in Sunday School work, and a Sunday School Festival or Rally was held every six weeks at Bethesda, when scholars repeated the "pwnc", or passage set by Griffiths.

In 1859 his flock contributed £53 as a gift in his honour, and secured the services of a Mr. Burton, a noted painter from London, to paint his picture. The event was organized jointly by Mr. W. Voss, one of the elders, Mr. G. Gower, who hailed from Norfolk, and the Rev. W. J. Ford, minister of Pilton Green and Parkmill. The festivities began with a sermon by the Rev. D. Howells, Swansea, in the morning of 8th of June at Ebenezer, Old Walls. The presentation was made in the afternoon at Bethesda, with Thomas Thompson, the late Lady Barham's son-in-law, presiding and paying tribute to William Griffiths. After giving an appropriate report concerning the occasion by Mr. Ford, the portrait was presented to William Griffiths by Mr. W. Voss. Further short addresses were given by the Revs. J. Whitby,

D. Howells, and W. Williams, of Swansea, and by Watkin Williams of Pen-clawdd. In his emotional response, Mr. Griffiths expressed deep gratitude, and for whatever blessing had been on his labours he gave all the glory to God's grace. An evening service, at which the Rev. W. Williams preached, closed the proceedings of a memorable day.

During 1859 and 1860 Wales witnessed a powerful revival, beginning in Cardiganshire through the labours of the Wesleyan Humphrey Jones and the Calvinistic Methodist, Dafydd Morgan. The year 1860 was also a time of spiritual harvest for William Griffiths in Gower, and

Revival year diary of Dafydd Morgan.

a typical diary entry is this: "May 31st, 1860. This forenoon we had our church meeting at Bethesda, and received ten new members, all, as far as we can judge, very hopeful characters. This is more than I ever received at one time in Gower before." However, his health was declining, and at the end of September that year Lewis Price came to assist him in his Gospel labours.

William Griffiths preached his last sermon on the text, Hebrews 10: 39, 'But we are not of them who draw back unto perdition; but of them that believe to the saving of the soul.' The date was Sunday, 28th of April 1861, and on the next day he fell off his horse, sustaining a serious injury from which he never recovered. During the following weeks in his affliction he had considerable peace of mind, combined with a heartfelt burden for the work of God's kingdom in Gower. He died peacefully on Sunday, 21st July 1861, leaning on his beloved wife of 35 years, Alicia.

What qualities justify referring to William Griffiths as 'The Apostle of Gower'? In what sense were his labours apostolic? Here are some considerations.

1. *He attributed everything of spiritual value in his life entirely to the grace of God.* Reviewing his spiritual condition the night before he was to be admitted to church membership at the Lord's Supper, he records his experience in this way: "1. I have often felt myself full of guilt and sorrow for my sin, and I have found rest to my soul in thinking of the sacrifice of Christ, and his salvation as revealed in the Gospel. 2. I have . . . given myself body and soul unto him, having no hope of being saved in any other way than through his free grace. 3. I know something of what is said in Romans 7: 21-22, 'I find then a law, that when I would do good, evil is present with me. For I delight in the law of God after the inward man.' 4. I have oftentimes found more pleasure in the work of the Lord, and especially in secret prayer, than ever I found in the ways of sin. 5. I feel a constant desire to live to the glory of God, and to be an instrument in his hand to help his cause. 6. I hope I know what it is to receive faith, repentance, and forgiveness of sins, according to the Gospel. 7. I do not know of any disagreement or ill-feeling between myself and any person in the church, or in the world."

2. He carried his family, his flock, and his neighbourhood on his heart at all times. One aspect of this was his regular practice to write to his son, also named William, on his birthday from the time he left home. The letters are full of good counsel, witness these sentiments: "First of all, have a jealous eye continually over the frame of your mind. The heart is like the chemist's laboratory, where many elements meet, where constant struggles between contrary principles take place: grace and sin, pride and humility, selfishness and self-denial, light and darkness, and all kinds of passions. Therefore endeavour to understand who is king within you . . . Secondly, be very discreet in the choice of company . . . Lastly, pray frequently . . ." There were other occasions when father advised the son in spiritual matters. "Grace is a principle that must be cultivated, because it is a new life in the soul that must be fed and nourished. Here is the grand difference between the nominal and spiritual believer. All the care of the first is about his outward profession, to live upright before men, and save himself from disgrace in the eyes of the world, while the latter feels daily another greater care of the inward motions of his soul." At no time did the father give the impression that Christian discipleship was easy. "I remember once", he confesses to his son, "I brought great guilt upon my conscience, the first year I joined the society, happening to be working for a few days with some strangers who were scoffers at all religion. One of them put the question to me whether I did not belong to those Methodists, and I answered in the negative, but this gave me such suffering that I determined ever after to avow my sentiments, and my public profession of the same, upon every necessary occasion."

3. He was a great Gospel missionary. He loved the Word of God, was convinced of its authority and reliability, enjoyed its promises, and lived by its precepts. His tireless preaching was evangelical and evangelistic, aimed at the conversion of sinners. The deacons at Bethesda bore witness to this in 1837: "His labours have been owned by the Great Head of the Church, both in the conversion of sinners and the edification of saints; indeed those who know him most possess the deepest conviction that his labours have been abundant and self-denying, and that his only object in those labours has been the glory of his exalted Master." On his fiftieth birthday Griffiths wrote: "I feel thankful to Him who thirty years ago opened my eyes to see my ruined condition, and, I trust, made me a new creature in Christ Jesus; and afterwards saw fit to employ me as a messenger of the Gospel of peace; has delivered me from the snares of sin, Satan, and the world, to this present day, and has overruled for my good all the trying events which have passed over my head." In his private diary he could record the "number of times I have preached from 1814 to the end of 1857, 12,536".

For the Sunday Schools Griffiths prepared 'pynciau', subjects or themes accompanied by a catechism, based on Scripture passages. One of these was published in 1841 with the title *Arweinydd i blant yr ysgolion sabbothol yn amrywiol bynciau y grefydd Gristionogol* (A Guide to several themes in the Christian Faith for Sunday School children). A seventh edition appeared in 1860. After a period of due preparation, there would be a kind of Sunday School Festival, with several churches attending and each in turn being catechized. Of one such occasion, he writes: "This forenoon the Sabbath Schools met at Bethesda, and there was a large congregation of attentive hearers. It was a beautiful day for them to come together from distant parts of the peninsula. All seem to feel interested in the subject, and many Scripture portions were recited by the schools. I hope that this mode of sowing the good seed is not in vain. The sword of truth is always sharp and powerful when it is wielded by the Spirit of God." The theme of one of the 'pynciau' was 'The character and example of Jesus Christ'. To the question, 'What are the examples of Jesus Christ wherein his people are to follow him?', there are 30 answers, each with a Scripture text or two for proof. Directions are given as to how to proceed: "The above subject is to be divided between the three Sunday Schools, to go round the whole twice; each class in each school to repeat only one head at one time. Bethesda Chapel, Nov. 2nd, 1835. Trinity school first, Rhosili second, Bethesda last. The following questions to be answered at the end by each school repeating together in one voice: Trinity. Question: What do you learn from these examples? Answer: From this we learn that none have a right to the name of Christ, unless they endeavour from the heart to walk in his steps. 2 Tim. 2:19-21; Rhosili. Question: How are Christians to follow the examples of Jesus Christ? Answer: Christians are to follow the examples of Christ by receiving of his spirit and grace, and continue in his fellowship. Bethesda: Question: What are the benefits which Christians receive in following the examples of Jesus Christ? Answer: Those who follow Christ shall not walk in darkness, but shall have light and life. John 8:12, 32."

4. *His passion for God and for godliness was intense and sustained throughout his life.* On his 64th birthday he writes this record in his diary: "Both in his providence and in his grace the Lord has been, and continues to be very merciful unto me, and every year seems to bring renewed evidences of his loving-kindness . . . Hitherto the Lord has not only preserved me in life, but has also made life pleasant to me. Not only has he preserved me as a member of his family, and a minister of his word, but he has also made my soul of late years more alive to my personal interest in his Son, and has, to a certain extent, given me the witness of the Spirit, that I am a child of God, and shall not come to condemnation, but shall inherit eternal life. I am frequently looking into this great question with all sincerity, and with prayer for the Divine guidance; and the conclusion that I generally arrive at is this: By the grace of God I am saved. I am born of the Spirit, and have my affections and heart set on things above. I shall not be lost in the perdition of the wicked . . . but shall by free and sovereign love, through the sacrifice of Christ alone, and by the saving and sanctifying work of the Holy Spirit in my soul, enter into the joy of my Lord . . . On the other hand, my conflict with sin is not less severe, nor my feeling of inward depravity less painful. I frequently find my heart so dead, and my thoughts so earthly and wandering in prayer, that I am obliged to pause in shame and silence . . . till I can recall my wandering mind into the sense of the *holy presence* of HIM before whom I bend my knees."

5. *He highly esteemed the good of the Church and worked fervently to bring saints to maturity.* Calvinistic Methodism was to him nothing other than New Testament Christianity. Its order was mutually beneficial to all churches, its priorities of itinerant preaching and society nurturing were

biblical and necessary. At a time of doctrinal integrity and ecclesiastical strength in his denomination, he was in the forefront, giving unqualified allegiance to its principles and aims.

The Inscription on William Griffiths's tombstone bears eloquent testimony to his character and labours:

> In Memory of the Rev. William Griffiths, Minister of the Gospel in the Calvinistic Methodist Connexion for nearly 50 years, and for most of that time Pastor of the Church in this place, who died July 21st, 1861, in the 73rd year of his age. His devout labours in this chapel, and throughout the Peninsula of Gower, as well as abroad among his Connexion, have been highly and extensively blessed, and have raised for him memorials of worth and usefulness that will far outstand this material monument. His indefatigable zeal in preaching Christ, in season and out of season, in planting the Gospel in benighted localities, his unwearied efforts for the instruction of the young, his holy character, his cheerful and benevolent spirit, will be held in lasting remembrance, and entitle him to be called 'The Apostle of Gower'. A life of constant application to work, and steady perseverance in his various plans of usefulness, with wise arrangement of time for their accomplishment, secured for him a good measure of influence and success in his respective spheres of labour. He rests from his labour, and his works follow him. 'They that be wise shall shine as the brightness of the firmament; and they that turn many to righteousness as the stars for ever and ever.'

Shortly after his death, Calvinistic Methodism had 974 churches, served by 409 ministers, with 91,462 members and 151, 817 attending Sunday School. It may be useful to review those elements in the denomination's strength which had maintained its integrity for well-nigh two centuries.

First was the evident blessing of God in providing great preachers whose evangelistic fervour and powerful preaching was blessed to the conversion of thousands of their countrymen. Beginning with Daniel

Rowland, Howel Harris, and William Williams, and followed by successive generations of men like David Jones, Llangan, Thomas Charles of Bala, John Elias of Anglesey, and Henry Rees of Liverpool, the denomination was remarkably blessed. Solid teaching from the pulpit was complemented by the provision of edifying literature, from Williams's hymns to Charles's *Christian Instructor* or catechism. Next must be mentioned the disciplined nurture of believers, added to the church by God's grace, by means of the 'society' meeting.

Denominational boundaries were extensively enlarged during several revival seasons. These occurred almost

THE
CHRISTIAN INSTRUCTOR:
OR
CATECHISM
ON THE
PRINCIPLES OF THE CHRISTIAN RELIGION.
BY
REV. THOMAS CHARLES, B.A., BALA.
(REVISED EDITION).
"That the soul be without knowledge is not good."—
PROVERBS xix. 2.

ENTERED AT STATIONERS' HALL.

CARNARVON:
PUBLISHED BY DAVID O'BRIEN OWEN,
C.M. BOOK ROOM.

Title page of Thomas Charles's 'Christian Instructor'.

every seven years during the eighteenth century, and frequently during the nineteenth, culminating in 1859 with a movement that spread throughout the Principality. Their rise, progress and achievements were so far beyond human agency that revival was seen as stemming solely from the divine initiative. This in turn confirmed the conviction that when the Church of God was in a state of slumber and decay, God's intervention should be sought as a matter of urgent prayer.

Thomas Charles of Bala passionately believed in and advanced the work of the Sunday schools. His efforts on their behalf stemmed from the conviction that Christianity is taught and not caught. In this he was not alone. Protestantism had vigorously promoted the use of catechisms for children, and Charles was following Griffith Jones's example of evangelism by education. Charles's article in *The Christian Guardian* for 1809 sets out the blessings that follow "associations of different schools . . . to be publicly catechised together." Lord Barham had for many years sent two guineas by way of annual subscription in support of the Welsh Circulating Charity Schools, and had served for a time as President of the Sunday School Society. There was an awareness that the knowledge imparted in Sunday school buttressed preaching by enabling the preacher to take for granted that his hearers could draw on a fund of salient biblical material. Furthermore, when children came to personal faith in Christ, what previously had been a mental store of knowledge would now fill out the meaning of their experience and provide a framework for advancing further in the school of Christ. Behind all this spiritual activity was a firm belief in the authority and reliability of the Bible as the written Word of God.

The fifty years that followed the death of William Griffiths proved to be years of growth for Calvinistic Methodism, which peaked as a result of the 1904-1905 Revival. It was a period when 'foundations were strongly laid' (Ezra 6:3) for the Pastorate churches. Their story will be told later in this book, and their resilience in the face of hostile influences bears ample testimony to the solid foundation laid by Griffiths and those who followed him. Victorian hypocrisy, Darwinian evolutionism, theological modernism and criticism of the Bible were making subtle but powerful inroads into the life of the churches. They would have a seriously detrimental effect on Gospel witness in the twentieth century. But as Moses witnessed on the mountain, even though the bush may be ablaze, it is not consumed. Christ will build His Church, and the gates of hell shall not prevail against it.

5. 'The winds blew, but the house did not fall': 1. Contrary winds

Eifion Evans

The story of the twentieth century for Christianity in Wales is the story of crisis and decline. True, the century started with the nationwide revival of 1904–05, and there were lesser spiritual harvests, as in the 1930s ministry of Dr. Martyn Lloyd-Jones at Sandfields, Aberavon, and in the late 1940s in North and South Wales. A movement of God's Spirit in Wales during the forties and fifties brought a spate of conversions, and the formation of The Evangelical Movement of Wales was a direct result of this. Nor should the mid-century effects of evangelistic crusades such as those of Billy Graham, and the growth of evangelical witness in the Universities and Colleges be forgotten. However, as the New Testament consistently warns, in this world there will be troubles and trials, the Church will always be under attack, and the love of many will grow cold.

Until mid-century the preferred name for the denomination remained 'The Calvinistic Methodist Church of Wales'. From that time the alternative name, 'The Presbyterian Church of Wales' became more fashionable, and this was an indication of the subtle shift in emphasis that was taking place in the Church's life. What had previously heralded a Methodist insistence on a personal experience of Christ, linked with a Calvinist understanding of the Christian Faith, became secondary to a title which gave prominence to order and government.

Within the denomination, the number of churches rose to 1054 in 1927, and of ministers to 997 in 1911. As a result of the 1904 Revival, the highest number of members was in 1905 and the mid-twenties with over 189,000, while the number attending Sunday School declined throughout the century from its peak of 222, 339 in 1905. In the half-century between 1947 and 1998, with the youthful generation of the 1904 Revival passing away, membership numbers declined from 166,

599 to 45,700, and Sunday School attendance dwindled from 98,497 to 9,071. During this period, the Bible had come under attack from various quarters. Its text was subject to scrutiny and criticism, its theology was vitiated by philosophical speculation, and its morality was revised in favour of the arbitrary ideals of man-centred humanism. The undermining of confidence in biblical integrity and authority filtered down from the theological colleges to the pulpit and to the pew. Preaching suffered as a result; the husk of oratory and 'hwyl' persisted, but the kernel of biblical content was seriously eroded. Congregations were being deprived of the Word of Life. There were still some preachers who believed the Bible and whose sermons faithfully explained and taught its message, but they were few in number.

The year 1933 was of enormous significance, a kind of watershed. It marked the demise of an older, biblically based, Christ-centred, salvation-orientated faith, and the adoption of a new order, in which the Bible was no longer central. Christ was marginalized by human achievement, and a social Gospel was deemed to be the hope of mankind. Personal dealings with God receded into the background, and the supernatural was viewed with scepticism. It was the year of an Act of Parliament that freed the denomination from its 1823 *Confession of Faith* and opened the way for union with other churches. The foundations of the denomination had been soundly laid; what winds battered the house with such ferocity as to bring about some serious breaches?

Firstly, the status of *The Confession of Faith* was changed from being the expression of the Church's doctrinal conviction to that of a historic document whose relevance lay in the past. This move stemmed from liberal theologians within the

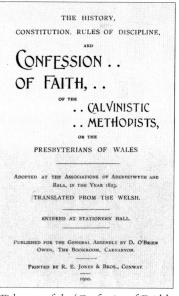

THE HISTORY,

CONSTITUTION. RULES OF DISCIPLINE,

AND

CONFESSION . .

OF FAITH, . .

OF THE

. . CALVINISTIC
. . METHODISTS,

OR THE

PRESBYTERIANS OF WALES

ADOPTED AT THE ASSOCIATIONS OF ABERYSTWYTH AND
BALA, IN THE YEAR 1823.

TRANSLATED FROM THE WELSH.

ENTERED AT STATIONERS' HALL.

PUBLISHED FOR THE GENERAL ASSEMBLY BY D. O'BRIEN
OWEN, THE BOOKROOM, CARNARVON.

PRINTED BY R. E. JONES & BROS., CONWAY.

1900.

Title page of the 'Confession of Faith'.

Church who were either unable or unwilling to accept precise doctrines such as a substitutionary atonement, justification by faith and the necessity for the new birth. Instead, they argued for more general, diffuse statements that acknowledged human 'moral consciousness'. Some evangelical ministers sought to check this drift away from biblical standards, arguing that its advocates were trying to gain control of churches which their own teachings would never have created, and which those teachings could never support. William Nantlais Williams, affectionately referred to as 'Nantlais', was minister of Bethany, Ammanford. He opposed the move by writing to the denomination's weekly newspaper, *Y Goleuad*, under the title 'Torri'r rhaffau', ('Breaking asunder the bands'). The material was also published as a pamphlet, and this was widely circulated. In the Church's courts he successfully argued the case for including in a proposed 'Shorter Declaration of Faith' a clear affirmation of belief in Christ's Deity, His Virgin Birth, atoning death, bodily resurrection and second Coming. In his 'Reminiscences', *O Gopa Bryn Nebo* ('From the summit of Nebo Mountain'), he acknowledged that it was something he received in 1904 that enabled him to persevere in the struggle. The need to make a more vigorous evangelical stand was also expressed by ministers and others meeting at Sandfields with Dr. D. Martyn Lloyd-Jones as Convener at the end of 1930. They were especially concerned to pray for revival, and to emphasize in their ministry such themes as the new birth, assurance of salvation and the pursuit of holiness.

The second major influence to affect twentieth-century Welsh Presbyterianism was that of the Ecumenical Movement. From the time of the Edinburgh Missionary Conference of 1910 this was a subject that had increasing prominence. One of the arguments in favour of the 1933 Act had to do with this very issue: the Act was intended to loosen doctrinal definition in order to facilitate union with bodies of diverging doctrinal positions. In 1948 the World Council of Churches was formed at Amsterdam, and the Welsh Presbyterian Church from that time has pursued its goals of assimilation and co-operation. The arguments for union most strenuously advocated were the scandal of division and the prospect of effective witness as one body. Opposition to this was expressed for several reasons. The World Council of Churches agencies supported revolutionary movements worldwide in their struggle for 'justice' and 'liberation'. Pronouncements were made on social issues, which should have been left to the expertise of politicians.

In Wales several initiatives sought to drive forward this kind of union: from the 1963 Report 'Towards Union', followed six years later by the proposal, 'Covenanting for Union', to the 1998 'Towards the Making of an Ecumenical Bishop in Wales'. The movement failed to recognize the need for a clear statement of the Gospel that was to be proclaimed, the faith that justifies before God, and the nature of the Church that would be created. Biblical unity is a reality where there is a common experience of God's grace in Christ, and a commitment to biblical teaching, but no such unity exists where these are absent. Significantly, Christ's prayer for the Church's unity comes after His prayer for the Church's purity: 'Sanctify them through Thy truth: Thy Word is truth' (John 17:17). It is salutary to remember 'The Dark Ages', when there was one, unified Church, but the truth was eclipsed, the way of salvation was corrupted, and generations were enslaved by soul-destroying superstition. Time and effort were invested in the pursuit of union at the expense of mission, so that at the century's close the denomination was in deep crisis with failing causes and depleted resources.

Meanwhile, maintaining a commitment to God's Word written became increasingly identified with holding an evangelical position, as distinct from the official, denominational stance of doctrinal indifference and ecumenical involvement. Departure from the Faith of the Methodist fathers over the last hundred years revolves around these two last-named features. As a result of this serious spiritual decline, evangelicals, who vigorously defended and propagated historic Christianity, were increasingly put on the defensive, and frequently found themselves at odds with the Church's policies. What was said of the early French Protestants could be said of the evangelicals, that they had "these five words continually on their lips: Gospel, Word of God,

Faith, Christ, Holy Spirit'. They were united in a shared experience of God's grace, a firm conviction of the Gospel as God's power to salvation, and a passion for Christ and for souls. They were at variance with most of their fellow members in their insistence on the priority and initiative of grace in salvation, on justification by faith not by works, and on the need for the Holy Spirit to bear fruit in God's work. Furthermore, few evangelicals were in positions of authority, and the denomination's stubborn defection from biblical truth, together with its fixation on a futile ecumenical ideal, seemed to present them with an impossible task. This constant conflict within the Church became intolerable for some of them, and on grounds of conscience they withdrew. Often they involved members of their congregations with them in their separation, and formed independent churches. They drew to themselves disaffected members from other Presbyterian churches, and from other denominations, but evangelical witness and influence within Welsh Presbyterianism was in some respects damaged, and certainly diluted, by their departure.

Other evangelicals remained, whether from timidity, hatred of schism, or in the belief that, given time and the blessing of God, a Church in declension may yet be restored. In this they saw themselves, like the Protestant Reformers, moderate Puritans, and their Methodist forefathers, as not setting out to create the Church anew, but to recover its early integrity and vigour. God had called them by His grace in spite of the compromised Presbyterian fold to which they belonged, and He could call others through them. As long as there was freedom to preach a biblical faith and fulfil a faithful, New Testament ministry, they held to the conviction that the Church must not only be reformed but is also always reforming. Church structures in and of themselves do not hinder or advance God's kingdom. Success lies entirely with God's Spirit, a pure Gospel, and a servant heart that seeks God's glory. In this world there is no perfection, but while this goal is unattainable, it should at least be pursued.

The twentieth century has been one of major national and social upheavals. It witnessed two World Wars, economic depression in the twenties and thirties, and a revolution in moral attitudes in the sixties.

A growing materialism together with an erosion of Christian standards and values has brought into being a society that is adrift from its Protestant moorings. The Christian edifice has been dismantled to an alarming degree. Those who now profess the Christian Faith face an ethos that can only be compared to that of the first century. Nothing can be taken for granted in a Christian sense. A secular state and a multi-faith society grant no favours. Only a robust adherence to the "faith once delivered to the saints", and a vigorous evangelism in dependence on the Holy Spirit can withstand this rising tide of unbelief and ungodliness. It was in these areas that the denomination was found wanting in the twentieth century. At the close of the Sermon on the Mount the Lord Jesus Christ speaks of two buildings, one built on sand and the other on rock. When the winds blew on the first it collapsed, having no foundation. The other stood firm because its foundation was strong. According to Christ the only secure foundation is submission to His Kingdom and to His teaching. With confidence that His kingdom is invincible and His truth unchanging, the Pastorate can face the challenge of the future with hope.

2. Tensions facing the Church

Jonathan I. Hodgins

As we embark on the twenty-first century, the term 'evangelical' has come to be adopted by a wide range of churches. All of these would profess to be Christian and yet would differ wildly on many issues, such as creation, the Sabbath, worship and their belief about what will happen at the end of the world. Broadly speaking however, an evangelical is a person who believes that the Gospel should be personally appropriated. This means that he or she has an experience of conversion and a developing relationship with God. An evangelical wants the Bible to impose itself on him, defining his lifestyle and opinions. An evangelical's witness is meant to be relevant. In Ellis

Wynne's *Gweledigaethau y Bardd Cwsg* (Visions of the Sleeping Bard) he describes a visit to church: "There I saw some whispering, some laughing; others eyeing young maidens; yet others surveying the dress of their neighbours from head to toe; some fighting and quarrelling about privileged positions, some asleep, others diligent in their devotions and some of these even were hypocrites." This is anathema to an evangelical because he wants the Gospel to be presented vividly in an exciting and thought-provoking manner. Moreover it should not be confined to Sunday worship. The Gospel should be communicated through the believer's activity within society.

That description could be applied to any orthodox Christian, as found in the Book of Acts and ever since. Why then use the term evangelical at all? The answer is that as the Church has expanded and become part of community life, all too often people regard themselves as Christians for such reasons as upbringing or nationality. Such make no claim to a personal knowledge of Christ, they show no intention of conforming to the Bible, and have no desire to share the Gospel message with others. Regrettably, this has not precluded such people from coming into membership, participating in the sacraments of the church and even assuming positions of leadership, often outnumbering the evangelicals within a church or denomination.

By the nineteenth century evangelicalism was doing a lot of good, in this country and overseas. For a time in Britain, Government policy was influenced by evangelicals like Wilberforce, Shaftesbury and Booth. Meanwhile overseas evangelicals were taking the Gospel to Africa, China and South America. In many ways this was a golden age for evangelicalism. And yet it was also its downfall. One commentator said of evangelicals, "Their first class brains died in the swamps of West Africa, and they left theological education to anyone else who liked to take it on" Whilst educating the next generation may have seemed less important at the time it is clear with hindsight that a grave mistake was made. "Those who liked to take it on" were either unqualified for the task or came from a more liberal position, persuaded by new interpretations that viewed the Bible as a product of tradition. For these reasons, by the end of the First World War, and in spite of various revivals across the country, evangelicalism had become a faction struggling to be heard within the mainline denominations.

It is a great mystery of course, that it is when we are at our weakest that God demonstrates his strength. In the decade following the Second World War, as a young Benjamin Tudor Lloyd was entering the ministry, God was reviving an interest in the evangelical tradition in three particular areas.

For those of us who rely on literature to help us prepare sermons, talks and Sunday school lessons it is difficult to think of a time without such resources. Nevertheless, before the 1950s it was

> **WHY DOES GOD ALLOW WAR?**
>
> A GENERAL JUSTIFICATION OF THE WAYS OF GOD
>
> D. MARTYN LLOYD-JONES
> (ASSOCIATE MINISTER OF WESTMINSTER CHAPEL)
>
> LONDON
> HODDER AND STOUGHTON

Title page of a Lloyd-Jones sermon.

very hard for ministers to access good literature with the result that they were spiritually malnourished. By the end of that decade however, groups like the Banner of Truth were publishing Puritan and other Reformed literature. A commentator notes that this "was heady stuff for many who had had a relatively thin doctrinal diet."

A second way in which God worked to revive evangelical interest was amongst students. Before 1939 Christian Unions were run by the Student Christian Movement, which had become very liberal in its outlook. Young people from evangelical churches were thus faced with a choice: to come under the influence of liberal theology or disassociate oneself from the Christian Union. In the 1940s and 50s however, the evangelical Inter-Varsity Fellowship [IVF], later to be known as the University and Colleges Christian Fellowship [UCCF] was formed. Its effects were profound, as D. A. Carson notes: "Historically, the impact of UCCF on confessional evangelicalism in the United Kingdom . . . during the last century is hard to exaggerate. It is difficult to think of many Christian leaders who were not shaped, in part, by the ministries of UCCF."

One of the problems faced by evangelical Christians in the first half of the twentieth century was marginalization, within their denominations and very often in their churches. At that time, men and women were looking for rational explanations and modern answers to their needs. It was a time of big questions and people wanted radical answers. In politics, diplomats hammered out alliances between the nations, while millions of people across Europe aligned themselves behind Marx and Lenin or Hitler and Mussolini to solve the economic problems of the day. As influenza swept across Europe in the post war period scientists sought cures for illness and delivered astounding technological advances. So when evangelicals offered up the Bible as a solution to the needs of men and women they were mocked or ignored not just by secular institutions but within their own church.

In 1954 however, the tide began to turn. Into the drab world of post war Britain came a young man whose dynamic preaching would attract thousands of people. Soon everyone would hear his name: Billy Graham, and he had already travelled widely telling people about the Gospel. People were interested in him and best of all, he believed the Bible! For years evangelicals had been shouted down for saying 'The Bible says', until they had become embarrassed to say it and now here was a man who had unashamedly made it his catchphrase!

For all the advances in evangelicalism in the post war period, one problem remained, afflicting large swathes of evangelical people of every denominational persuasion. It sapped the energy and disheartened the most optimistic of people. It was denominationalism. Many evangelicals worked away, trying to reform institutions from the inside, others gave up, deciding to simply "work away in their small corner". After all what was the alternative?

On the evening of October 18th 1966, addressing members of the Evangelical Alliance, in Central Hall, London, Dr. Martyn Lloyd-Jones sowed seeds for just such an alternative with a plea for evangelical unity. He began by examining the reasons for the existence of evangelicals. He saw the term 'evangelical' as synonymous with 'Christian', in that evangelicals fitted the description of Christians in the New Testament. The formation of the Evangelical Alliance was an

D. Martyn Lloyd-Jones in conversation with John R. W. Stott at the meeting of The Evangelical Alliance, October 18, 1966.

example. Looking back over history he saw that evangelicals within different denominations had seen the need to gather together to form "alliances, movements and societies." In other words those who called themselves evangelical found themselves isolated within larger denominations. As these denominations moved towards anti-evangelical agendas, evangelical people found strength in forming groups. Whilst this may have been pragmatic, it created problems.

Firstly, the emphasis on para-church activity led to the accusation that evangelicals were against Church unity. Whenever a church committee met, evangelicals always came across as negative. They were synonymous with opposition, disagreement and counteraction, so that whilst evangelicals professed belief in the Church as a body of believers, in practice they gave the impression of being more interested than anyone else in maintaining the integrity of their different denominations. After all evangelicals appeared happier in para-church organizations. They spent most of their time in fellowship with people outside their denominations returning only to defend the ancient standards of denominations and denounce their leaders.

Secondly, by organizing themselves into para-church groups, the doctrine of the Church had to be sidelined. In order to maintain the unity of groups like the Evangelical Alliance or the Evangelical Movement of Wales, "the authorities in the movements . . . always pointed out [that] if you discuss the doctrine of the Church you will cause divisions." This is fairly obvious. The Presbyterian view of church government, with its emphasis on presbyteries, is quite different from the Independent view of personal autonomy or the hierarchical Anglican system. Debating these issues could only cause controversy. To preserve the *status quo* evangelicals were called on to remain within their denominations as preservatives but to enjoy fellowship within movements.

To Lloyd-Jones this was not acceptable. As he looked out from the podium at the ministers gathered before him he asked them, "Are you content with a kind of paper church? The church surely, is not a paper definition. I am sorry. I cannot accept the view that the church consists of articles or of a confession of faith . . . A church consists of *living people.*" What merit was there, he continued, in maintaining a denomination if the majority of its members did not hold to its distinctives? The denomination might remain, the buildings might still be seen as churches, but it was no longer the New Testament Church. The days of fighting were over; what was the alternative?

One option was to accept the ecumenical move towards one territorial church. Evangelicals could band together and form an 'evangelical wing' of the church, hoping that "others would see the wrongness of their ideas and the rightness of ours" Lloyd-Jones saw this as a miserable outcome. "Does the church consist of people who are unconverted and who need to be converted? Surely not!" To argue from that position would be to argue "that if you succeed in bringing together a sufficient number of dead bodies they will come alive!" Instead, Lloyd-Jones wanted to return to the church of Acts 2: 42, where we are told that believers 'continued steadfastly in the Apostle's *doctrine* [or teaching], in fellowship, and in breaking of bread, and of prayers.' In other words, it is not character, or temperament or effectiveness which qualifies but what we believe that is of paramount importance. Only when that is established can a church truly exist.

Furthermore, Lloyd-Jones was not speaking of evangelical ecumenicity as representing the 'finished article'. However, unity he argued was not something to be worked for but something to be perfected. "Unity is not something which exists, or of which you can speak, in and of itself. It is always the consequence of our belief and acceptance of this great and glorious doctrine of God, who has provided in His Son the way of salvation, and who mediates it to us through the operation of the Holy Spirit. That is the basis and the nature of Christian unity. It must never be thought of except in terms of this great background, this essential doctrine."

What then, was he advocating? To Lloyd-Jones the situation as it was, was inconsistent. He began by arguing that most people's affiliations to denominations were an accident of birth. ("I was born an Anglican", or "I was born a Methodist"). What made a person a Christian was not denomination but salvation, regardless of affiliation. Secondly, evangelicals were being inconsistent with the very thing they claimed they were loyal to. Many evangelicals were arguing that as long as they had personal liberty they were happy to remain in the mainline denominations. Yet for many, their denominations were built on corporate lines. The Presbyterian system, for example, is a belief in the wider church, there is no independence in Presbyterianism. By ignoring the leadership, evangelicals were incongruent to themselves. And then thirdly, evangelicals were inconsistent in their evangelism. To the 'man in the street' the contradictory situation was, at best, "difficult to understand". Finally, the preacher turned to the positive side of his proposition. He appealed to those present to act in the tradition of the Reformation and consider the benefits of coming together not occasionally, but always. He recognized the difficulties that would be faced, and the fears, but appealed to those listening to recognize that they lived in a "great turning point of history . . . a day of glorious opportunity"

Developments from the mid-1950s have demonstrated that it was a time of much tension, of heart-searching and decision-making, for evangelicals within the Presbyterian Church of Wales. They were resolved differently according to conscience, circumstances and opportunities as making up God's providential dealings with individuals. At the beginning of another century these tensions continue and will be worked out in the context of the existing, worshipping congregations. Through these churches God's Church will, like the bush ablaze but not consumed, continue. The winds that blow will only vindicate the foundation of faith, conviction and commitment that has already been laid, firstly by William Griffiths, latterly by B. Tudor Lloyd, and presently by Iain B. Hodgins.

6. 'Houses full of good things'

Eleanor Jenkins

1. Bethesda, Burry Green

List of Ministers

William Griffiths	1824–1861	Thomas Williams	1922–1927
Lewis Price	1860–1877	D. Stanley Davies	1929–1931
Samuel Price	1877–1889	David Evans	1932–1936
Evan Rowland	1889–1893	D. Stanley Davies	1943–1946
W. Jenkin Jones	1893–1899	Medford W. T. Lloyd	1950–1956
Thomas Williams	1899–1910	B. Tudor Lloyd	1956–1994
Howell J. Lewis	1910–1922	Iain B. Hodgins	1995–

Soon after Lady Barham's arrival at Fairy Hill in 1813 she discovered that a few Christian believers were preparing to set up a small Meeting House on the edge of the Green, just a quarter of a mile from her new home. Finding that she and they held views in common, she asked if they would allow her, at her own expense, to erect a considerably larger building than they had proposed. This was Bethesda Chapel as we now know it, and this little company became its first membership. A manse was also erected by Lady Barham, and this at one time was called Barham House. They, the original 'church without a building', considered themselves Calvinistic Methodist as did William Griffiths, the evangelist that Lady Barham had invited to work in Gower. He continued to live and minister in Gower after Lady Barham withdrew her patronage in 1822. Two years later he was ordained, Lady Barham's son restored that patronage, and Griffiths became resident minister at Burry Green. In 1855 at Griffiths's request, Lord Barham gave the Gower chapels, built at Lady Barham's expense, to the Calvinistic Methodist Connexion.

Burry Green, Trinity and Old Walls were under the care of Rev. William Griffiths until his death in 1861, when he was succeeded by Rev. Lewis Price who had come as his assistant in 1860. We read in the minutes of the District Meeting of the Gower Churches for 1873 that Burry Green was considering the election of elders. Sunday School work is often mentioned in these minutes and the children of Burry Green attended the Sunday School anniversaries held jointly with the other churches. Another subject which was discussed at length was how to improve congregational singing, and in 1878 it was agreed to give every encouragement to hold prayer meetings in private houses.

The District Meeting in 1880 "called the attention of our ministers and teachers to the lack of order and devotion manifested by many of those who frequent our Religious Services and it was resolved that an effort be made to induce those who are in the habit of standing in groups outside the various chapels before the service commences to enter in due time and to cultivate a respectful attitude especially whilst the devotional part of the service is carried on viz. to stand whilst singing and to kneel when praying." In April 1886 John Rogers of Kennexstone was appointed secretary to the District Meeting, and also in that year papers were read by the ministers on the importance of the Prayer Meeting, the Church Meeting and 'the best means of securing better attendance at our Sunday morning services'. It was agreed to send visitors to the various Sunday Schools to stimulate and inspect the schools.

A hundred years after Lady Barham came to Gower, Deane Gordon was born in Tyle House Farm, just across the Green from the Chapel. He 'never remembers not going' to chapel for he was carried there before he could walk. Deane's earliest memory is of sitting in the back seat on the right with a crowd of other little boys – a row of girls occupied the seat in front. These 'babies' were taught by Miss Elizabeth Williams who was succeeded by Jenny Tanner from Stembridge who also played the organ – once it arrived! Burry Green first had an organ about 1914 and even then there were complaints from Captain Badcock for one, who did not want to worship 'by machinery'.

On the other side, under the window was a class of older boys taught by Mrs. Lewis, the minister's wife, but by the time Deane would have been old enough for this class it had disappeared. The adult women met in the vestry with Emlyn Rogers's father, while down at the front of the chapel was a class of men led by John Rogers's father – these were the 'theologians' who 'went into things deeply'. It was straight to this class that Deane graduated in his teens and where he listened to the men debate. In particular he remembers an old gentleman called Kit (Christopher) Williams who worked as a carpenter for the Bensons at Fairy Hill, and who had experienced a remarkable conversion. When it was time to finish, a 'banging on the seats' brought the ladies filing out of the vestry.

During the First World War a young man called Edgar Nottman came to work for the Bensons at Fairy Hill. While there he came under the influence of Rev. Howell J. Lewis, minister at Burry Green from 1910-1922 and subsequently offered himself as a candidate for the ministry.

Water and electricity came to Burry Green during Rev. Medford Lloyd's ministry (1950-1956). Putting in these modern conveniences was a big undertaking for which the Chapel borrowed money from the Loan Fund. At about this time Mr. Sidney Heath, who lived next door in Burry Cottage, began lending his beautiful gardens to the Chapel for annual garden parties. These were wonderful affairs which

Sunday School outing, 1946.

continued for many years. The proceeds were at first for Chapel funds and then increasingly, for overseas missionary work, especially for "our" hospital at Durtlang in Northern India.

Despite the advent of electricity, Gower could still be a dark place as Rev. B. T. Lloyd discovered on his arrival:

When I came to Burry Green in 1956 there were no streetlights, and even the bulb in the telephone kiosk outside the chapel was not functioning; when it was replaced a few weeks later, I couldn't sleep for the glare! On my first trip from Swansea after a District meeting, the bus made its way through these parts in total darkness. When a fellow passenger got off the bus in the pitch dark just before coming to Kennexstone Moor, in order to cross the fields to his home, Mount Pleasant, the comment of the Swansea conductor was, 'How can he live in the middle of nowhere!' I got off at Kennexstone Cross, in order to walk to Burry Green and save a twenty minute wait in Llangennith. I hardly noticed the bus going round the corner, but I soon wished I had watched carefully, because I could not see a thing. There was the sound of rushing water somewhere near, but there was nothing to be seen, just blackness. Then I remembered a tip I had picked up somewhere: no matter how dark the night, there is usually a slight difference between the sky and the top of a hedge, which is even darker. And so it was. Gradually I could pick out just where the hedges were, and I made my way home.

Once at home, things were, at first, not always much better:

It was as a dyed in the wool suburbanite I moved into the Manse, and it was lonely. There was not one bungalow in Burry Green then, and the neighbouring properties were an ivy covered ruin on one side, and the chapel and graveyard on the other. When my parents went back to Cardiff after the Induction, I felt the truth of Mr. Stanley John's remark to me, 'I wouldn't like to live in an empty house.' 'It isn't empty when I'm there,' I said, but it was a debating point – it did feel empty. To make matters worse, I had never liked going into an empty house. For one thing, as the Plaza and Gaiety cinemas in particular had instilled into me, empty houses are rarely empty; enter them with torch, and in no time, to the crash of an orchestral chord, the circle of light focuses on a prone figure with a knife in his back. Such not very alive characters tended to fall out of wardrobes too when least expected. Should a torch be avoided, and the light switched on, it is only to reveal patiently seated there some big men of definitely ill intent. I sympathise with the little girl in Old Walls who was making her way to the bathroom in the dark. When her parents called out to ask why she hadn't put the light on, she replied, 'If there's someone there, I don't want to see him.' No, I can't say I liked empty houses, probably because of those comparatively innocent films. What the result is of today's TV violence and horror, I dread to think. Moreover, when I went to bed that first night on my own in Burry Green, I discovered that old houses are not silent places. I woke up in the early hours, and heard the eerie sounds of old beams and floor boards creaking and cracking, the wind making strange sounds in the chimney, and possibly the sound of screech owls which at that time were plentiful. I definitely felt uneasy, and said to myself, 'If this is how it is going to be, you are going to have a pretty miserable time here.' And then a verse of Scripture came to my mind. It was verse 4 of Psalm 34: 'I sought the Lord, and He heard me, and delivered me from all my fears.' So it proved for me; I turned over, and went to sleep, quite at home in the Manse, groans and creaks and all. For that, I continue to be thankful. 'Praise be to You, O Lord; teach me your decrees', (Ps. 119:12).

Seven years after the induction of Mr. Lloyd in 1956, Burry Green celebrated its 150th Anniversary and for this important milestone Rev. Dr. Martyn Lloyd-Jones was invited to preach. Bethesda itself would have been too small for the numbers anticipated and after much deliberation a large marquee was erected in the field behind the chapel. People came in hundreds. Even now, as we approach the bicentenary, the time when "Dr. Martyn preached in the tent" is clear in the memory of those who heard him. Mr. Lloyd remembers the preparations:

We expected very good congregations on the Sundays, and so it turned out. As a matter of fact, on the second Sunday every nook and cranny of the chapel was occupied – floor, gallery, vestry, Lady Barham's Room, and the porch. I was forced to remain in the pulpit throughout the service, sitting behind Mr. Phillips. What of our plans for the Thursday? Christian people in West Glamorgan would want to hear Dr Lloyd Jones, and would come in large numbers, as they would not have to neglect their own churches in order to do so. My suggestion was that we hire a marquee which seated 900 plus standing room. This alone would cost £150 – no small amount in 1963. Money was not losing its value then as it did later, even though the cost of living was more expensive than in 1956 when I first came to Gower. At that time I could go into town with ten shillings in my pocket, that is, 50p, and know that I could buy a couple of gallons of petrol if needed, and also fish and chips. Suez had made a big difference to the cost of living by 1963, but a pound would still be a comfortable amount in one's pocket. Finding £150 for a marquee was a challenge therefore, and the congregation wavered before coming to a decision. Then Mr. John Rogers spoke up. 'Where's our faith?' he said, and went on to propose successfully that we commit ourselves to the marquee; but we still had to find the £150 to pay for it. A day or two before the marquee arrived, Glyn Rogers came in from the fields at the end of the day, and suddenly remembered that in his pocket was a letter for his father. The postmen had given it to him that morning in order to save himself the long walk to the house. The letter, totally unexpected, was from Mrs. A. O. Morgan, the widow of an Aberystwyth doctor, who was a grand-daughter of the Rev. William Griffiths, the first Calvinistic Methodist minister of Burry Green Chapel. She expressed her pleasure at coming across the programme for the Anniversary celebrations, but regretted that at her advanced age she was unable to be with us. She had enclosed a cheque for £150 as a contribution towards the expenses!

On the first occasion that Mr. Lloyd held a Christmas Morning service in the little vestry there were about ten people present, and it was followed by coffee in the Manse next door. As time went on a few members from Old Walls joined the group and the whole idea took off and grew from year to year. The service moved into the Chapel and by the time he retired the gallery was also in use on Christmas Morning. During the 1970s the congregation's interest in foreign mission was marked by a visit from Dr. Biakmawia, of India. Mr. Lloyd ministered at Bethesda from 1956 to 1994, and he was followed a year later by the Rev. Iain B. Hodgins. The Christmas service has continued to the present day, with these two ministers taking it in turn, and we are glad to see members from all the chapels and friends from far and wide gathering to praise God on that occasion.

Dr Biakmawia's visit to Bethesda.

The Rev. Geraint Fielder recalls coming to Burry Green in the late fifties with a group of Christian students on a campaign. They had been invited by Mr. Lloyd to work in the area and camped for the week in the garden of a ruined cottage next door to the Manse, where Stuart Grove's bungalow now stands. Although it was warm summer weather, Mr. Lloyd remembers that the nights were clear and cold and it was decided that the women should sleep in the chapel vestry. As well as Geraint Fielder who became a good friend to Burry Green, preaching often at Anniversary Services over the years, the group included Miss Mair Davies who has since been a church worker in Patagonia. The aim was to evangelize the area and the students held meetings in Burry Green Chapel and in the open air as well as visiting the various farms and homes giving out invitations and selling Christian books.

Although the number in membership has declined in recent years, the congregation is now strengthened during the summer months by holidaymakers coming to Gower from every part of the country. It is good to have fellowship with them all. The Sunday School mentioned so often in the District Meetings of the last century has continued, almost without a break, to the present day, although the children now travel by car or bus rather than walking. There is still the involvement with the other Sunday Schools for outings and weekends away and the present group of children love to sing and take part in the annual Singing Festival at Tabernacle, Pen-clawdd. A further development begun during Mr. Lloyd's ministry and continued by Mr. Hodgins has been the monthly Family Service for which the parents join us and which are led by our minister. We trust that, in the words of the District Meeting of 1874, it will all be "to the furtherance of the Redeemer's cause in the land."

2. Ebenezer, Old Walls

List of Ministers

William Griffiths	1823–1861	John Badham	1904–1910
Lewis Price	1860–	J. C. E. Morgan	1911–1924
J. Wyndham Lewis	–1867–	R. E. Ellis	1925–1928
Daniel Williams	1872–1877	Stephen Jones	1928–1934
D. M. Davies	1879–1888	Alfred J. Moore	1934–1937
D. M. Rees	1889–1892	Medford W. T. Lloyd	1950–1956
Clement Evans	1893–1896	B. Tudor Lloyd	1956–1994
W. D. Rowlands	1898–1903	Iain B. Hodgins	1995–

When Mr. William Griffiths ceased to be Lady Barham's school-master and preacher in Pilton Green following the re-organisation of her chapels on Congregational principles, a new Society, "formally united with the Welsh Calvinistic Methodists", was formed in the house of Mr. William Voss, Nicholaston, on 26th of March, 1823.

William Griffiths writes in his *Gower Memories* that "in the summer of 1823 two new places of worship were opened . . . Old Walls Chapel on the north side, a Preaching Room fitted up at Overton on the south side." Rev. William Williams takes up the story, "There was at Old Walls, near Llanrhidian, a chapel which had been built by the Wesleyan Methodists some ten years before this time, but which had fallen into a very dilapidated state in consequence of having long gone out of use. The people who raised it had left the neighbourhood, and had given it up to the owner of the ground on which it was built. The place was taken for a period of twenty-five years, for £20 down and £1 per annum rent, Mr. Griffiths and his friends taking the repairs upon themselves. On the day that this bargain was made, Mr. Griffiths says in his journal, 'I feel very happy that we have one place of worship in Gower. This far has the Lord provided. O for a grateful heart!'"

The widely scattered members numbered 37, but "scores were obliged to stand outside" when Mr. Griffiths preached in Old Walls on the Sunday evening prior to the lease being agreed. The first Communion Service was held on Sunday morning, July 27th 1823, at which the officiating minister was the Rev. David Charles, Carmarthen, hymn writer, and brother of the Rev. Thomas Charles of Bala, one of the founders of the British and Foreign Bible Society. In August 1824, Mr. Griffiths was ordained in Llangeitho.

Financially and in other ways the times were hard, but the situation was greatly improved when, having inherited the almost deserted Burry Green and Cheriton chapels, Lord Barham invited the Rev. William Griffiths in November 1824 to become their minister. This was accepted on conditions laid down by the Calvinistic Association which met in December 1824. Among the conditions were these: Mr. Griffiths should be accountable to the Calvinistic Methodist (C.M.)

Connexion, and that the doctrine preached and the discipline exercised should accord with the C.M. Confession of Faith and Rules of Discipline. Burry Green then became the "central home" of the Society where the Sacraments were administered and new members received. Preaching Services continued elsewhere as before. In 1852 Old Walls Chapel was rebuilt.

Mr. Griffiths continued as minister of the three chapels until his death in 1861, when he was succeeded by Mr. Lewis Price, who came as his assistant in 1860. In 1864 Zion, Llangennith was built, and for a few years the precise pastoral details are not clear. It is certain that for a brief period prior to 1870, including the year 1867, Old Walls and Trinity were under the care of the Rev. J. Wyndham Lewis. He lived in 'Llwynderw', afterwards used as the Manse for the Old Walls and Penuel pastorate, and ideally placed on the road between the two chapels.

It is interesting to note that when the District Meeting of the Gower Churches was established in 1873, the first secretary appointed was Mr. Richard Dunn of Leason. The minutes record that in May 1875 an anniversary meeting for the Sunday Schools of all the Gower churches was to be held at Ebenezer, Old Walls. This event took place annually and in 1876 the children from Penuel and Old Walls were to be examined by Rev. Lewis Price, minister of Burry Green, while the Old Walls minister, Rev. Daniel Williams questioned the Burry Green, Trinity and Llangennith children.

In April 1882 permission was requested to renovate Old Walls and then in 1886 " it was resolved that a kind message be sent to the church at Ebenezer, Old Walls to renew the holding of its church meetings which are considered so essential for spiritual intercourse and edification." After the churches were transferred to the English-speaking Presbytery in 1891, "it was agreed that, if desired, a Presbytery meeting be held at Old Walls in the autumn. There was considerable enthusiasm for the visit of Presbytery and a brake was secured for the benefit of delegates and the churches urged to entertain them well. The brake met the delegates at Killay. Mr. Rees and Mr. Rowland were asked to select the preacher."

Sunday School play 1939.

This pastorate of Old Walls and Penuel lasted from 1872 to 1910, and enjoyed the ministry of some who became leading figures in the Denomination. In 1911 Old Walls called the Rev. J. C. E. Morgan to be minister, a Manse was built in 1922, and this arrangement continued until 1937. A vestry was built in 1930 during the late Rev. Stephen Jones's ministry. He was followed by Rev. Alfred J. Moore who stayed in Gower for just three years but is remembered for encouraging the Sunday School scholars to take the Scripture exams. Eileen Hutin remembers that they would walk down to the Manse after school for extra lessons with Mrs. Moore, and on at least one examination day, Mr. Deane Gordon from Burry Green was their invigilator, walking up and down between the tables as they wrote. Old Walls was without a minister from 1937 to 1950 when the four North Gower chapels were linked in a single pastorate.

In 1950 Rev. Medford Lloyd became their minister and many in Old Walls have happy memories of his work with the young people in particular. He already had links with the area, having spent college vacations potato picking with the Johns at Tyrcoed Farm. Mrs. Audrey Williams and Mrs. Eileen Hutin remember that having started a weekly Young People's Guild, "he was very good at producing plays, and was a very practical man, able to make a switch board and provide all the stage lighting for the Guild plays which proved so popular before television came on the scene. His 6 years at Old Walls certainly made an impact on us." So popular was Medford with the younger members of his congregation that on one occasion Eileen Hutin remembers going with John to another chapel where their minister was taking the service. They soon realised that they were listening to the sermon they had already heard on the previous Sunday. On the way out, Medford greeted them, "Serves you right for following me around!" He also knew his older members well. The 'sewing circle' was often more popular than the Sunday services and when introducing a keen member of that circle, to the newly arrived Tudor Lloyd, Medford was heard to comment, "Take a good look at this lady, because you're not likely to see her again very often."

John Hutin's friendship was later extended to Rev. B. Tudor Lloyd whose induction took place in November 1956. Calling at the Hutin's home one evening, Mr. Lloyd had enjoyed a game of darts with John, using the board which hung on the back of the parlour door. When the time came for John to leave for a darts match in *The Welcome*, Mr. Lloyd asked, "Can I come too?" John thought this definitely would not do, but Eileen has often wondered since what the consequences might have been if the minister had been allowed to accompany John.

Mrs. Audrey Williams, elder at Old Walls writes, "I think it was about 1951 when we started to do plays with the children of the Band of Hope. Once when we were performing *Dick Whittington*, Mrs. Pritchard and Mrs. Averil Grove had made little rat costumes complete with tails for the smaller children. These little rats had to fall asleep on the stage and remain in that same position until someone clapped, then jump up. This they did, all except my little Rosemary who was only about three years old and she had really gone to sleep! Then on another occasion, there should have been a clap of thunder. John Markham was in charge of the tin sheet – and there was a hoarse whisper from the wings, "John, the thunder!"

The 1955 cast of 'Happiest days of your life'.

In those days, Old Walls and Burry Green held separate prayer meetings during the week, entailing a two mile journey for the minister which could at times be hazardous. Mr. Lloyd recalls: "One dark night, when cycling down past Dunraven to the Old Walls Prayer Meeting, I had a close encounter with ponies. Unexpectedly I was in the midst of them. There was a sudden clatter of hooves, a blow to the bicycle, and I was picking myself up from the road with a sprained wrist, but able to carry on. On inspecting the bicycle the next day, I discovered that the kick had dented the substantial frame of the 1956 Raleigh just above the chain case (yes, chain case!) How that hoof missed my shin I do not know, but I have a good idea of what damage it would have done."

Mrs. Audrey Williams recalls Mr. Lloyd visiting them just after he arrived in November 1956. He had called into Newton Farm first where Averil and Ernie lived with their daughter Kathleen. He said Kathleen had asked him to draw a cat (she would have been about two and a half years old) and when she saw the drawing she burst into tears. Mr. Lloyd used to say that he had no illusions about being an artist after that! However, they found out later that she had wanted a picture of a cat lying down and he had drawn one standing up! Audrey comments that the children always felt at home with Mr. Lloyd. She remembers another incident when he had been to visit elderly Mrs. Bladen in a nursing home in the Uplands. There were four patients in her room. Mr. Lloyd had taken her a packet of sweets and as he gave them to her on leaving, three pairs of eyes followed him out of the room. He told Audrey that he never visited that nursing home again unless he had four of everything!

It was while Mr. Lloyd was minister in 1973 that the members at Old Walls celebrated the 150th Anniversary of their chapel. The preachers for the occasion were Rev. J. Glyn Owen of Westminster Chapel, London, and an old friend of the pastorate, Professor Rheinallt N. Williams. It was also for that Anniversary that Mr. Lloyd wrote the brief history of Ebenezer, Old Walls, from which many of these notes have been taken.

In 1994 after 38 years as the 'Gower minister', Mr. Lloyd began a well-earned retirement and the occasion was marked by a service held in Old Walls on his birthday, 28th April. It was attended by a host of friends and good wishes were expressed by representatives of all the chapels. He was presented with a cheque, a picture and a reclining chair in which to enjoy his retirement, which, fortunately for us, has not proved too restful as he has continued to live in The Manse at Burry Green, to attend meetings and to preach in churches all over the Presbytery and beyond.

Old Walls has kept up the tradition, begun in 1891, of entertaining District and Presbytery Meetings and the ladies have become noted for their apple tarts. In recent years two other lunches have become popular traditions: one at Christmas when the children of the local primary school sing carols in the Chapel, and one on Good Friday following a joint morning service in one of our churches. The collection at these lunch meetings is always given to charity. In 1998 Old Walls celebrated their 175th Anniversary for which an attractive booklet was produced with memories of older members, a history of the cause and the building, and various organisations.

When Mr. Lloyd had announced his retirement, Mrs. Averil Grove was heard to exclaim, "It's all right for you, but what is going to happen to us?" What happened to us in God's will and in answer to Mr. Lloyd's prayers, and ours, was that in 1995 Rev. Iain B. Hodgins came from Cambridge with his family to be minister of the Gower Pastorate. It is typical of the relationship between the two ministers that Mr. Lloyd wrote in the Old Walls Anniversary booklet in 1998, "Our prayer is that Mr. Hodgins's hard work, in which he is stoutly supported by his family, may be crowned with blessing from on high."

3. Penuel, Llanmorlais

List of Ministers

William Williams	1844–1851	D. M. Rees	1889–1892
Charles Bowen	1851–1854	Clement Evans	1893–1896
David Saunders	1856	W. D. Rowlands	1898–1903
Watkin Williams	1857–1860	J. Badham	1904–1910
Thomas John	1861–1862	J. H. Owen	1911–1917
Morris Morgan	1864–1871	B. T. Evans	1920–1929
Daniel Williams	1872–1877	Lewis Morris	1937–1969
D. M. Davies	1879–1888		

About the year 1842 there came into the district a farmer by the name of William Davies, and he occupied Llanelen until the end of his life. He and his wife were of a religious turn of mind and therefore became interested in the spiritual life of the neighbourhood. At this time there was no fixed place where the people could congregate for worship.

They held meetings in the houses, and also in the open air. The people seemed to be without any outstanding person able or willing to undertake the task of endeavouring to establish some fixed place of worship. On the site of the present Chapel people used to congregate and hold meetings. One old man by the name of David Bennett who lived at "The Close", was a regular attendant. He always brought with him a bench which served as seating accommodation for part, if not all of the congregation. It is also interesting to know some of the old hymns that he always gave out: 'Not all the blood of beasts on Jewish altars slain, Could give the guilty conscience peace, or wash away his stain'; and also, 'Not the righteous, sinners Jesus came to call'.

The owner of Llanelen where William Davies farmed, was a Col. Cameron. He also owned the Bryn Farm known as Caecenwyn, and William Davies being a tenant of his, the approach was very easy. In company with a Samuel Eaton, who lived at the farm, William Davies succeeded in securing a piece of land on which to build the Chapel. The land was given free but there are no legal documents relating to it. The cartage of materials for the construction of the building was carried out by Messrs. Davies, Eaton and others.

When the Chapel was erected, a day school was carried on during the week and religious services on Sunday. The teachers at the day school were named Bennett and Morris: the latter was the grandfather of the late Mr. John Rees, one of the oldest leaders and a secretary of the Church. At this time the services were School in the morning, Preaching Service at 2.30, and Prayer Meeting in the evening. This form continued until 1870 when the Rev. Daniel Williams came, and Penuel and Old Walls were joined.

The chapel built in 1843 was formed in conjunction with Tabernacle, Pen-clawdd. The growth of the cause, the distance from Pen-clawdd and the language difficulty made the building of another chapel inevitable, and Penuel was opened in 1844 under the ministry of Rev. William Williams. He could say, "On Wednesday nights I hold a class in Penuel. Generally between 50 and 60 young people come there to meet me." The masonry work was constructed by David Lloyd, who subsequently left the neighbourhood. He was assisted by his nephew, Phillip Williams, who, at an early age, sailed for America, where he spent the remainder of his life. The church was enlarged in 1866 while the Rev. Morris Morgan was minister. During the time of enlargement, week-night services were held in the most conveniently situated private houses. Mr. and Mrs. Edward Matthews were very sympathetic and the Sunday services were held in Tir-Coch barn.

When the next minister, Rev. Daniel Williams, came in 1872, Penuel and Old Walls formed a joint pastorate and the new minister lived at 'Llwynderw'. As a point of interest, on the day that Mr. Williams set foot in Gower, he came to Killay by train and Mr. Sam Davies, the son of William Davies, coming home from Swansea on Saturday, brought him with him in the market trap, putting him off at Welsh Moor. He was then directed to Llwynderw.

Rev. D. M. Davies was minister from 1879 to 1888, and in 1886 the church was rebuilt. During the building period, week-night services were held in the most suitable private houses of the neighbourhood while the Sunday services were again held in the barn at Tir-Coch, and the Sunday School in the barn of Mr. John Davies, Bryn. During the time of the second chapel, crowds of people came to the Anniversary services, and many could not enter the building. At one Anniversary, the Rev. Thomas Rees preached a powerful and memorable sermon, outdoors, on Zacchaeus. The preacher was dramatic and the occasion was remembered for a very long time.

Rev. Clement Evans was minister from 1893 until 1896 and conducted a wonderful Bible class in each church which was greatly appreciated and referred to often. His successor, Rev. W. D. Rowlands, came in 1898 and he and his wife were the first occupants of the new Penuel Manse which had been built in 1897. Rev. J. Badham was minister during the great Revival of 1904, when Penuel shared in the blessings. As a result, the membership doubled and both prayer meeting and services were well attended. Mr. David Edmunds who died in 1907 was a deacon of Penuel at this time. His outstanding achievement was the Young Men's Prayer Meeting held on Sunday mornings at 9.30am and over which he presided. It was at one of these Prayer Meetings that the Revival touched Penuel. William Jeffreys, who came from a Baptist background became associated with the church at Penuel after his marriage. He was at first an ordinary member until, on one unforgettable Sunday morning in the young Men's Prayer Meeting he received a great spiritual blessing. From that moment he was eloquent in prayer and church meetings and he maintained that high level of experience until his death in 1938. He was a deacon for twenty-five years.

Mr. Badham was followed by Rev. J. H. Owen who had been born in Newtown and trained at Bala College. The previous six ministers had also had the care of Old Walls but by the time that Mr. Owen came from Westgate, Pembroke, Penuel had become a separate pastorate. Then came Rev. B. T. Evans who died at the early age of fifty-four. He preached the truth without fear or favour and occupied the pulpit almost to the end. Mrs. Evans, who had endeared herself to the church, lived in the Manse for some years, doing much good work with the children. The church, however, was now without a pastor for eight years during which time attempts were made to unite with Crofty under the same minister, but without success.

Mrs. Megan Beynon Jones remembers that her grandparents would drive in a horse and trap from Llythrid to Penuel where the horse would be given grazing in a field next to the chapel. Her parents however attended Old Walls and it seems that this was typical. There were very few houses near Penuel and people came from a distance, many walking up the long hill from Wernffrwd. As time went on more chapels were built and younger generations found places of worship nearer home. Unlike Crofty which was growing fast, no new building took place near Penuel and the congregation became smaller.

Mrs. Gwyneth Robert grew up in Penuel and remembers that the Sunday School during those years in the early thirties was taught by Miss Bet Edmunds and Miss Sarah Lizzie Jones. When Rev. Lewis

Morris came in 1937, his wife taught the older children, who still remember her telling them, "You've got to give your heart to the Lord." Mr. Morris also organised plays which were put on in the chapel and there was a Prayer Meeting and Band of Hope. The Whit Monday tea was the highlight of the year with tea, bread spread with salt Welsh butter, and cake being served in the chapel on boards laid across the pews, followed by races in the field adjacent to the Chapel. The next day everyone went down to Tabernacle for the Singing Festival. Sadly, Mr. Morris died in a car accident on the Jersey Marine Road in January 1969, when returning with his wife from an ordination of elders in Mission Hall, Neath. He proved to be Penuel's last minister. He was sadly missed, numbers declined and the chapel finally closed its doors in 1988.

4. *Tabernacle, Pen-clawdd*

List of Ministers (incomplete)

William Williams	1844–1851	D. M. Davies	1888–1911
Charles Bowen	1851–1854	R. G. Davies	1914–1924
D. Saunders	1856	W. E. Williams	1928–1958
Watkin Williams	1857	Meidrim Thomas	1962–1976
Thomas John	1861	Meirion Thomas	1979–1983
Morris Morgan	1864–1971	B. Tudor Lloyd	1990–1994
W. D. Williams	1872–1881	Iain B. Hodgins	1995–
Hugh P. James	1883–		

In 1815 Lady Barham appealed to the Welsh Calvinistic Methodist Association for a minister. Mr. Rees Jones from Anglesey was chosen for this work and the new minister was stationed at Pen-clawdd. During the first two or three years of his ministry he preached and held Sunday School at a dwelling house near the centre of the village until a chapel was built. Bethel, near the site of the present Congregational Chapel, was completed and was opened in 1818.

Tabernacle, Pen-clawdd.

Rees Jones, ordained at the Methodist Association in 1818, retained his pastorate at Bethel after Lady Barham severed her connection with the Calvinistic Methodists in 1821. His ministry covered a period of fourteen years and was the means of inspiring many with Calvinistic teaching by the time of his death in 1829. Now that Bethel had lost its Methodist Pastor the members became concerned about their future, and ultimately called an Independent pastor, with the result that as many as forty seceded and chose to begin a little society in the village of Pen-clawdd, the nearest Methodist cause being at Moriah in Loughor.

Mr. Thomas Roberts records that "for some time we met to worship in a room of an inn in the village." The inn referred to was the

"White House" from which they moved after about seven months to "the Hall", a substantial farmhouse in the west-end of the village. Describing their services there, the Rev. William Griffiths wrote, "I preached in Pen-clawdd in the room where our friends meet for divine worship ever since they have been deprived of their chapel. They have hired a good capacious room, and it was quite thronged with attentive hearers."

For seven long years the little society continued to worship in their meeting place, often under most adverse circumstances. These difficulties, however, they successfully surmounted, until the Monthly Meeting of the denomination, satisfied that here was really the nucleus of a strong Methodist cause, requested the members to look around for a suitable site upon which they might build a chapel. "After much doubt and great difficulty," wrote Mr. Thomas Roberts, "we procured the land and a suitable chapel was built upon it." The first Tabernacle, which occupied a site near to that of the present chapel, was opened on June 3rd 1836. The cause was generously supported during those early years, although a debt of £80 still remained in 1841. Consequently the society felt that it could not adequately maintain a pastor, and for eight years the pulpit was supplied mainly as the result of the inclusion of Tabernacle with Loughor and Goppa (Pontarddulais) in a preaching circuit, each chapel being visited in turn by the minister.

Rev. William Griffiths tells of a proposal at the Monthly Meeting to ask all the Sunday Schools in the county to raise "a fund among themselves for supporting a missionary in Gower." With the prospect of being assisted, as the result of this proposal, in maintaining a minister, the society at Tabernacle prevailed upon Mr. William Williams of Penllyn, near Cowbridge to come and minister among them. His work there began in 1844.

Considerable progress was made in the following years and especially during the ministry of Rev. Morris Morgan who came in 1864. A marked increase in attendance at all the places of worship in Pen-clawdd led to alterations and even rebuilding of several chapels. In 1867 the friends at Tabernacle sought permission to extend both chapel and manse which they were able to do despite doubts expressed by the Monthly Meeting over the plans and cost involved. The ensuing debt was paid off by 1876. This wave of enthusiasm can be attributed partly to an increase in the population of the village as people came there seeking work in the coal, copper and lead industries. Another factor was the outbreak of cholera in 1866 which made many people anxious for the first time about their spiritual well-being. The membership of Tabernacle, for example, increased from 67 to 109 in just two years from 1864 to 1866. The new Tabernacle was completed and opened in 1867.

The ministry of Rev. D. M. Davies (1888-1911) saw the opening of the new vestry in 1892. By 1908 the membership had risen to 347 and it was again felt that a new and better chapel was needed. Following a request for financial support, £700 was given and work on the third Tabernacle began. The beautiful new chapel, which with the organ

Rev. D. M. Davies in the previous pulpit.

reached a total cost of £5,400, was opened in 1911, but with a huge debt confronting the members. The paying off of this debt is still remembered by present members. Mrs. Audrey Howell remembers that her grandparents would raise not one pig, but two, the second being sold to support the Chapel. In the same year, 1911, Mr. Davies died after 25 years at Pen-clawdd. During that time he had held office as Moderator of the Association in the South, a reminder that in those days Tabernacle belonged to the Welsh Presbytery. This continued until 1980 when the chapel moved over to join the English-speaking Glamorgan Presbytery West. Mr. Raymond Williams remembers that services in Tabernacle were never completely in Welsh. Even in the days of William Griffiths the language had presented a difficulty. Having preached at Pen-clawdd in 1819 he wrote in his diary, "Had some liberty in the English, but the people made such a disturbance between the two languages that I was quite uncomfortable and could hardly speak in the Welsh. A very indecent habit they have of going out many of them after the English part is over." Soon after that time Rev. William Williams wrote that "Pen-clawdd stands where the two languages, like two seas, meet and produce a current over which it is difficult for a preacher successfully to sail." By the early years of the next century the language had become less of an issue and Rev. W. E. Prytherch of Swansea remarked upon "the harmony that prevailed at Tabernacle between the Welsh and English languages, a duality unique in the Methodist Connexion."

Rev. D. M. Davies was succeeded in 1914 by Rev. R. G. Davies who remained throughout the First World War, and continued to preach occasionally at Tabernacle after leaving for Llandeilo in 1924. Isaac John Griffiths who was later to become chapel treasurer, recorded in his diary how the minister prayed for him on the eve of his departure for that War. It is interesting to learn that in those days Chapel House, which housed a succession of caretakers until the retirement of Mrs. Beryl Leyshon in recent years, was situated, not behind the Chapel, but on the opposite side of the road. Family and friends would gather there after the Chapel service and lively discussions would ensue about the day's sermons and other related topics.

Alicia Griffiths.

William Griffiths.

Three ministers: Jonathan I. Hodgins, B. Tudor Lloyd, Iain B. Hodgins.

Bethesda, Burry Green congregation.

Ebenezer, Old Walls congregation.

Tabernacle, Pen-clawdd elders.

Trinity, Cheriton congregation.

Zoar, Crofty congregation.

B. Tudor Lloyd when Moderator of the Association in the East.

Connexional Seal on the gallery facing the pulpit at Tabernacle, Pen-clawdd.

Mr. William Jenkins's Sunday School class, 1950s.

At the time of the centenary of the cause in 1936, the minister was Rev. W. E. Williams. He is remembered among other things for his diligence in visiting his members. If someone had been absent on Sunday, he would be at their home on Monday morning and if they were out, they would return home to find a chair standing on the kitchen table as a clearly understood message from their minister. Should he not have visited for a while, his habit was to throw in his hat before entering. Doors were seldom locked in Pen-clawdd in those days!

Mr. Williams was to remain minister through the war years which followed. Many allied troops were stationed in what is now Graig y Coed, and would parade to church in their Black Watch tartan or G.I. uniform. A number of girls from the Chapel were to marry servicemen, among them, Ethel Williams, Carrie Howells and Ethel Evans. Many of the leading members of Tabernacle were schoolteachers and consequently were an asset in linking the children with the Chapel and the day-school with the Sunday School. Mr. Ivor Jenkins, Precentor at Tabernacle, is remembered not only for his lovely singing voice, but for the way he invoked prayer at the gates of the munitions factory situated on the point at Crofty during World War Two.

Rev. Meidrim Thomas, became minister in 1962 and during his time Tabernacle was in a joint pastorate with Bethel, Gowerton, both churches then being in the Welsh Presbytery. He is remembered as a keen herbalist whose remedies are still occasionally recommended today. He was also known to have painted the house in his hat and coat!

In 1976 after the retirement of Mr. Thomas, it was agreed that Zoar, Crofty should join the pastorate to call Rev. Meirion Thomas of Llanidloes, who accepted the call in 1979. His induction service was held in Tabernacle in October of that year. In 1981 there were snow blizzards and it was discovered that the roof space at Tabernacle was full of snow. Many volunteers hurried to clear it away but in the process the lathe and plaster ceiling was damaged and fell down. Tabernacle left the Welsh Presbytery to become part of the English-speaking Association in the East in 1980, and Mr. Thomas left for Crickhowell in the Brecon and Radnor Presbytery in 1983.

It was not until 1990 that Tabernacle was added to the churches of the Rev. B. Tudor Lloyd, to become part of the Gower Pastorate. His

Celebrating the Coronation at Tabernacle, 1953.

ministry at Pen-clawdd lasted only three years before he retired, and he would, of course, have been thinking and praying about the future of the pastorate for which he had cared for over forty years. It was during this time that he began visiting Tyndale House at Cambridge for brief study breaks and became acquainted with the Bursar, Rev. Iain B. Hodgins and his family. Mr. Hodgins had spent eleven years in the Presbyterian ministry in Gwent and, in Cambridge, had been instrumental in beginning the Presbyterian Church where Mr. Lloyd worshipped while on holiday. He discovered that Mr. Hodgins was in a position to consider returning to the pastoral ministry and began praying that God would, in time, call him to Gower.

In making these links and introductions, in God's providence, Mr. Lloyd was following the pattern of Rev. Rees Jones who, almost two hundred years earlier, had put forward the name of William Griffiths for the work in Gower. While minister at Burry Green, Rev. William Griffiths himself had visited, preached and cared for the church at Pen-clawdd, encouraging them constantly to seek ministry. Mr Lloyd has done the same and the church is grateful to God for calling such men to Gower and for their ministry over so many years.

5. Trinity, Cheriton

List of Ministers (incomplete)

William Griffiths	1824–1861	Stephen Jones	1928–1934
Lewis Price	1861–	Alfred Moore	1934–1937
J. Wyndham Lewis	–1867–	Medford Lloyd	1950–1956
Thomas Williams	1899–1910	B. Tudor Lloyd	1956–1994
Howell J. Lewis	1910–1922	Iain B. Hodgins	1995–
Thomas Williams	1922–1927		

An early picture of Trinity comes from the 1863 *Memoir of William Griffiths* by William Williams. The year is 1817, and William Griffiths has arrived in Pen-clawdd, only to find that Lady Barham no longer

Trinity, Cheriton.

needs him there. He still feels deeply that the Lord has work for him to do in Gower although it seems there is no option but to return home. Mr. Williams writes, "It was not, however the will of Providence that he should leave. A 'door' was 'opened', although at the time it appeared but for a short season. Lady Barham had built a little Chapel in a village called Froglane, between Cheriton and Llanmadoc, on the shore of the Burry Estuary, and about seven miles south-west of Pen-clawdd. This small building, long, low, and thatched, half chapel (for it had a pulpit), and half schoolroom (for it had no pews), was called 'Trinity Chapel'. A school was held here on week-days, and sermons preached on some evening in the week, and once, and occasionally twice, on the Sabbath. Mr. Griffiths, during his months of suspense at Pen-clawdd, went down frequently to preach at Trinity, and some times was 'very much helped, though the people seemed exceedingly wild'."

Teachers for Lady Barham's schools were chosen as much for their piety as for their ability, and the evangelistic purpose of the schools is made clear by the equipment provided which included Bibles, Testaments, catechisms and tracts. The same book records of Cheriton, that "the school-master's name was Philip Gwyn, a most earnest and devoted young man. But his health was indifferent. Lady Barham kindly gave him a month's holiday to recruit his strength, sending Mr. Griffiths in the mean time to supply his place at the school. The young man, however was never able to return to his duties. His illness increased, and after a few months he died. Mr. Griffiths was appointed schoolmaster at Trinity; with the additional duty of preaching there, as well as at other places in the surrounding neighbourhood." William Griffiths was to remain in Gower, though not actually in Cheriton, for many years and when he was finally appointed minister in 1824, the *Memoir* notes that, "Great was the joy of the people of Gower upon being permitted with their beloved pastor to take possession of Bethesda Chapel, as well as its little appendage, Trinity. Mr. Griffiths had continued to preach occasionally in the latter, up to the time of his dismissal from Immanuel Chapel; and a few days before that event took place he had preached there his 'farewell sermon' from the words, "hitherto hath the Lord helped us;" and now, when he again entered the little place after an absence of nearly two years, he took for his text the same motto, "*hitherto* hath the Lord helped us."

The grouping of the Gower churches into pastorates has changed several times over the years, and for a few years after the death of William Griffiths it is difficult to know whether Trinity was linked with Burry Green or with Old Walls. It is certain that for a brief period prior to 1870, including the year 1867, Trinity, Cheriton as well as Old Walls were under the care of Rev. J. Wyndham Lewis.

Trinity is mentioned several times in the District Meeting. In 1873, along with Burry Green and Llangennith, the church sought permission to appoint elders, and in 1876 the children were taking part in the Anniversary of the Sunday Schools held that year at Old Walls. Also in 1876 when the instruction of children was under discussion, we read that, "Family Religion was introduced by Trinity and received the support of the meeting."

The Rev. Thomas Williams (inducted in 1899) wrote, "This Chapel, which is one of the smallest in the Connexion, was built in 1817, at a probable cost of £150. It was then stone-floored and straw-thatched, and seated with rude backless benches. In 1867, it was completely renovated, at a cost of £150. It was now slate-roofed, ceiled, wood floored, and fitted out with modern seats – altogether a very neat little Country Chapel." During his ministry, the little chapel, built on a leasehold site, was claimed by the landowner when the lease ran out. The Chapel and the site were bought for £150, and Mr. Williams comments, "Now this would be a great hardship in the case of any church, but it is especially so in this case. Trinity has always been very weak – has never averaged much more than 20 members. The cause is linked with Burry's Green and Llangennith under one pastorate, and has lately borne with them the cost of renovating Burry's Green (1904) at a cost of nearly £400, and Llangennith (1908) at a cost of nearly £200. It is the only Noncomformist place of worship on the northern side of Western Gower. It supplies the villages of Llanmadoc, Cheriton, and Landimore. We could not for a moment entertain the idea of letting the cause become extinct. We feel confident that many who love the Lord Jesus Christ will gladly help this little Bethel in difficulty, and we most earnestly appeal for sympathetic aid. The Chapel is now in need of considerable renovation, but the faithful few cannot face such a burden alone."

The money must have been found for the cause continued, still linked with Burry Green and Llangennith. Mr. Deane Gordon was born a few years after the above appeal was made, and remembers attending the annual teas and concerts at Trinity. As a young boy he went to Llanmadoc School, now a ruin at the top of the steep hill leading down into Cheriton village. On such occasions, always in May, there would be no playing of rugby or other rough games in school, because he and others, no doubt, would go to school dressed in their best clothes. At the end of the afternoon, they would run down the hill to the tea which awaited them in the chapel. Two tables would be placed across the seats, the children served first, then the adults. It was a very plain tea, he remembers – cake, bread and butter and possibly some jam. The evening, on that day, was taken up with a concert in the chapel for which the village people turned out.

Trinity was linked with Old Walls during the ministry of Rev. Stephen Jones (1928-1934) and in his letter to the pastorate in 1928 he wrote: "Even if we are few at Trinity (24 members that year), we thank God for the help and strength we receive through the week-night services. The church meeting has been well attended throughout the winter." It is interesting to read that by 1931 the membership had risen to 30 and Mr. Jones writes that the "Church at Cheriton continues to make progress and we rejoice to know that a Young People's Guild has been formed there from which we hope to receive good results. The friends at Trinity deserve our congratulations for the way in which they beautified the Sanctuary of the Lord during the year and we are most grateful for all gifts received during the renovations."

After the time of Rev. Alfred J. Moore (1934-1937) Trinity, like Old Walls, was without a minister for thirteen years, but, by the end of 1939, the membership, which had been falling, had risen again to 25 and the Secretary, Mr. G. T. R. Taylor, was able to write with thanks-giving, "Our membership has increased, and the attendance at the week-night services has shewn a marked improvement. The financial side of the church is very satisfactory, and we now hope to have the Church renovated, the front re-plastered and a new porch erected."

From 1950 to 1956 Trinity was one of four churches under the care of Rev. Medford Lloyd and in 1956, Rev. B. Tudor Lloyd was inducted to the same pastorate of Old Walls, Cheriton, Burry Green and Zion, Llangennith. He writes,

I remember as though yesterday cycling to Cheriton for the first time. From Kennexstone across the moor was not quite the level ride it looked, and there was a double benefit in stopping to chat to the road men who were working on the gutters. The few minutes' conversation of that afternoon was the beginning of long-lasting friendships I value still, though the friends themselves have passed on. Then back on the bicycle for what I thought would be quite an uneventful ride, but not so. All of a sudden, totally unexpected, there was a glorious view of the Burry Estuary. It took my breath away. It is still a wonderful view, but now its glory is revealed more gradually, because the saplings of that day have grown into substantial trees partially concealing the vast sweeping view of dune and sandbank, river and sea, hill and shore, some of them distant. I felt something of the hymn writer's 'awesome wonder' when he wrote 'How great Thou art' in praise of God the Creator of all.

The late Miss Dorothy Taylor, organist at Trinity, used to recall meeting the new young minister in Cheriton on that day or soon after, and asking how long he thought he might stay in Gower, to which he replied, "Until I'm known as 'Old Tudor Lloyd'." Mrs. Hilary Spencer remembers that Mr. Lloyd did most of his visiting on foot or cycling from Burry Green over the years. When she first attended Trinity in 1957, she thought the man taking the service must be a student, not the minister, as he looked so young. There were about fifteen members then, many of them men, and quite a few children although there was no Sunday School.

This began in September 1980 when Mr. Lloyd asked Cathy and Eleanor Jenkins who were members at Burry Green to meet with a small group of children on Sunday afternoons. The Sunday School was welcomed and encouraged by the members of Trinity and continued until 1992 when parents asked if they could bring their children to Burry Green where the children met at the more convenient time of 10am. This joint Sunday School has continued to the present day, still enthusiastically supported by members of Trinity, who now run a mini-bus to collect families from Landimore, Cheriton and Llanmadoc and bring them to Burry Green. Family Services are also held jointly and, when Trinity is the venue, these are now followed by a church lunch in the hall across the road. The annual Pastorate Summer Supper which has raised many hundreds of pounds for Christian charities is also hosted by members of Trinity. Although numerically weak all through its history, this little church is very gifted and still makes a

Trinity Sunday School in the 1980s.

contribution to the work of the pastorate quite out of proportion to its size.

An example of such a contribution is the North Gower Christian Project which is now in its second year. In conjunction with Burry Green, Trinity initiated the call of Mr Jonathan Hodgins as Church Community worker in the area. Supported by these two churches and with a grant form the Mission Board, he has been able to work in local schools and with the churches, contacting and building relationships with children and families. In this second year the other three churches in the Pastorate have joined the Project together with Moriah, Loughor. Jonathan has now been ordained and the churches are blessed and encouraged through his ministry and witness.

6. Zion, Llangennith

List of Ministers

Lewis Price	1860–1877	Thomas Williams	1922–1927
Samuel Price	1877–1889	D. Stanley Davies	1929–1931
Evan Rowland	1889–1893	David Evans	1932–1936
W. Jenkin Jones	1893–1899	D. Stanley Davies	1943–1946
Thomas Williams	1899–1910	Medford W. T. Lloyd	1950–1956
Howell J. Lewis	1910–1922	B. Tudor Lloyd	1956–1971

Zion, Llangennith, was built in 1864. It stood at the top of the hill near Pancras (or Pains Cross) Moor, reputedly the site of an ancient battle, and was better known locally as the Pancras Chapel. In those days the pastorate of Cheriton, Burry Green and the newly opened Zion were under the ministry of Mr. Lewis Price who had originally come as assistant to Rev. William Griffiths a year before his death in 1861. The new fellowship was in fact a 'church plant' or branch of Burry Green. For this reason, the list of ministers assumes that the church was under the same pastoral care as the 'mother' church. No less than thirty people from five hill farms were walking the few miles to Burry Green to worship three times each Sunday, and it was sensible to build a place of worship nearer to their homes.

Llangennith belonged to the Calvinistic Methodist District Meeting, and its meeting in June 1874 was held at the chapel. By that time the Sunday School children were to take part in a joint Anniversary meeting at Old Walls. Subjects such as Romans 8 and Acts 1 and 2 were chosen. These were prepared by the children and during the meeting held two years later they and their friends from Burry Green and Trinity were examined by Rev. D. Williams, minister at Old Walls. In 1881 it was agreed by the Meeting to send a message to Burry Green, Llangennith and Trinity expressing the desirability of holding an evening service occasionally at Burry Green Chapel. In June 1886 we read of the renovation and repair of the building at Llangennith, and then in 1891 it was agreed that a request be sent to transfer the churches to the English-speaking section of the denomination.

By the early 1900s Mr. Deane Gordon believes that Zion was probably the strongest of the three churches, "with a good number of big families, mostly hill farmers: the Jones's of Barraston, Beynons of Tankey Lake, Clements of Penmynydd, and the Williams's". Like the other Gower Chapels they held an annual tea and concert in May and Deane remembers that "they fixed up a little fire grate under the hedge on the other side of the road and it was there that the water was boiled for tea-making. Once tea was over, they all played games in the field behind the chapel until 7pm when the concert began."

By the time of Rev. Medford Lloyd (1950-56) numbers had fallen and Mrs. Audrey Williams remembers that attempts were made by Presbytery to close the little chapel. "Medford looked round at all the ministers present in Presbytery that day and said, 'How many of you had 100% of your members present at last Sunday's service?'" It seems that he alone could make this claim about attendance within the Presbytery churches at that time.

Sad to relate, Zion Chapel ceased to be a place of worship in 1971, leaving Old Walls, Burry Green and Trinity Chapels as the continuing pastorate. Robert V. Barnes, a lay-preacher, has precious memories of Zion; one of them concerns the organ. "The building consisted of a simple single room with a porch on the landward end. The pulpit was at the seaward end of the building and there was a small communion area below the pulpit. The organ, which was of the foot pedal variety was located to the north of the pulpit in the corner. It was an interesting American organ in that it had a little dial on it which indicated the amount of air the organist had succeeded in putting into the bellows. For the closing service in 1971, the church was reasonably full with support from the other churches in the pastorate. I was very conscious of playing the organ in the presence of Mr. Deane Gordon, the organist of Burry Green and a far superior musician to me. The hymns went well as I pumped furiously at the organ to get the air through. It was evident from the outset that the elderly instrument was leaking very badly and it was a struggle to get enough air into it to make it play. In the last hymn it finally succumbed, and pump as hard as I could I was unable to keep enough air in the organ to sustain the notes. As we sung our way through the last verse of the hymn the organ quietly gave up the ghost and we ended singing unaccompanied. It seemed poignant, somehow, that the organ should die with the cause." Mr. Barnes also highly esteems preaching and fellowship experiences at Zion: "The church was greatly used by God as 'a beacon on a hill' to proclaim the Gospel. Its witness to Jesus Christ in the village extended over more than a century and it lives on in the memories of all those associated with it. I thank God for the great opportunity Zion gave me to develop as a preacher; for the privilege of having known that small but precious number of Christians who worshipped there regularly right up to the end, and above all for the delight of knowing Zion's wonderful pastor, Rev. Tudor Lloyd – the modern day Apostle of Gower – and a true successor to William Griffiths, the first Apostle of Gower."

Following the closure, the chapel was sold and the remaining members of Zion transferred either to Old Walls or to Burry Green. The elder, Mr. Evan Jones, with his brother, John, came to Burry Green where they proved as faithful and enthusiastic for the cause as they had ever been.

7. Zoar, Crofty

List of Ministers

Rev. D. M. Davies	1888–1911	Meirion Thomas	1979–1983
W. A. Roberts	1911–1913	B. Tudor Lloyd	1985–1994
E. T. James	1926–1935	Iain B. Hodgins	1995–
Melville B. Thomas	1944–1947		

As far back as 1829 there was a fellowship of Calvinistic Methodists at Crofty and Wernffrwd for both Rees Jones and William Griffiths were in the habit of conducting religious services in various dwelling houses in the area. Some forty years later the Primitive Methodists, known locally as the 'Ranters', established themselves in Pen-clawdd. Members of Zoar, in later years, acknowledged their connection with the Primitive as well as the Calvinistic Methodists and pointed to the evangelizing work of Mr. Davies, the 'teaman' and Mr. Hadwin, a shop owner, both of Pen-clawdd. These men would come to Crofty and preach on the very spot where Zoar now stands, in a corner of a field known to the locals as 'the Gags' (its real name was Gag Fawr). A cart was often borrowed from the Crofty Farm across the road as a pulpit for the preachers.

By the 1880s the centre of activity for the Crofty Methodists seems to have shifted to the 'Haggard' cottage next to the Pencaerfenni Farm, which has now been demolished and replaced by a number of dwelling houses. In a lean-to building by the cottage was a weavers' factory run by Mr. James Morgan. It was here that the Calvinistic Methodists of the village held their Sunday School.

In the years immediately before 1883 Crofty grew rapidly as a village. Mines opened all over the area and the population expanded. It became clear to Methodists in Crofty that a building of their own was not only viable but essential to the carrying on of the cause. In December 1883, it was reported in *The Treasury* that a schoolroom was to be erected in Crofty in connection with Tabernacle, Pen-clawdd. The following year 'Zoar' was opened. We assume that the opening took place in May of that year because Anniversary services have been held in that month for as long as present members can remember. Unfortunately there appear to be no records of this event which was so significant for the village.

It is, however, known who the 'moving spirits' were in the founding of Zoar. Mr. David Williams, the last of that breed of village tailors who were renowned story-tellers, had been involved in the Sunday School work for over 50 years. His namesake, David Williams of Llanmorlais, was another prominent church member. Others were Robert Guy, William Tanner and John Williams, all of Crofty. The present church owes much to the work of these stalwarts in the 1870's.

Although initially known as a schoolroom the building was recognised as a branch of Tabernacle as early as 1888. This brought Zoar under the ministry of Rev. D. M. Davies, then minister of Tabernacle and previously of Penuel and Old Walls. At the time of the Revival in

1904 it was reported in a newspaper that boys had broken into Crofty Chapel. Further investigations showed that rather than simply being vandals, they had been caught up with the spirit of the Revival and were holding a prayer meeting.

The cause at Crofty continued to prosper and by 1906 it was found necessary to enlarge the chapel. The repairs and extensions were on such a scale that the chapel was virtually rebuilt. A new feature, welcome in this windy spot, was a heating system. Reading through the Chapel accounts it can be seen that this system was not entirely trouble free! The builder responsible for this rebuilding work was Mr. David Thomas, assisted by 'Young Davy' both of whom were elders of the chapel.

An important day in the history of Zoar was 23rd August 1908. On that day it was incorporated into a church. In subsequent years the membership grew steadily and in 1911 the church was able to call its first pastor, the Rev. W. A. Roberts. He was able to secure the freehold of the land so that the building was entirely owned by its own trustees. When he left for Australia in 1913 the membership stood at 81, which by 1925 had grown to 103. The ministry of Rev. E. T. James at Zoar began in 1926, lasted until 1934, the year which also marked the fiftieth anniversary of the founding of the chapel. At this time the membership stood at 115 while the Sunday School was regularly attended by 80 pupils. In order to celebrate the anniversary, the chapel was renovated at a cost of £115. On the great day, two services were held, both well attended. It was during the evening service that Mr. David Edmunds of Llanmorlais, secretary of the church, gave the history of the cause in Crofty, an account to which this article owes much.

Mr. Edmunds is also remembered to this day as a Sunday School teacher who encouraged his pupils, including Margaret Eynon-Davies, to learn the whole of 1 Corinthians Chapter 13 by heart. Margaret remembers that in those days, her aunt, Mrs. Carrie Williams lived on Llanmorlais Cross and kept a little shop attached to the bungalow. Auntie Carrie would 'keep the ministers' who came to preach and who would often stay for the weekend, but she would refuse to let them pay for anything from her shop on a Sunday, even if they had run out of cigarettes! The goods might be handed over but payment was not allowed until Monday morning. Another well-loved Sunday School teacher was Mr. Leigh Oakley. Mrs. Gwyneth Morris remembers being in his class and that he had also taught her mother in earlier years. He would take his class out on day-trips, the most exciting being two days in London where they stayed with Mr. Oakley's sister and niece. Annual Sunday School outings were also made to Barry, Porthcawl, Tenby and even Aberystwyth.

The church continued without a pastor during the years leading up to the Second World War, and was glad to welcome several American soldiers to services while they were stationed in the area. Evacuees also came to the area and were welcomed in Zoar. The three year ministry of Rev. Melville B. Thomas of Pencoed began in 1944, and he was instrumental in setting up a Building Fund for the erection of a new Manse. After the war, but while Mr. Thomas was minister, Zoar began holding an eisteddfod in the chapel on Christmas night.

Some Zoar members with the Rev. Melville B. Thomas.

Competition was hot in all the age groups and small velvet purses were presented as prizes to the winners in each section. Rev. Lewis Morris would come from Penuel as adjudicator for the recitations. The big event of the night was the octet section for which three groups of singers would normally compete after weeks of secret practice. The annual Whit Monday walks have been held for as long as anyone can remember, always culminating in a tea in the chapel for which boards were placed across the pews. These 'tables' were necessarily high and Mrs. Gwyneth Morris remembers as a child of about four reaching up for a piece of plain cake only to discover that she had seed cake in her hand which she disliked very much, but nevertheless had to eat. Soon after Mr Thomas had moved to Maryport, Cumbria, the church was saddened to hear that both he and his wife had been killed in a road accident.

During the years which followed, when the church was without a minister, the weeknight meeting continued with outside help. In the early seventies Rev. Russell Williams of St. Mellons drew up a list of subjects and various men were invited to speak. Twice a year, Rev. Neil Richards of Neath would come for a month to give a series of talks. Later, during Rev. B. Tudor Lloyd's ministry, Rev. Ken Williams, a former missionary to Nigeria, began to attend and was then prepared to take over and lead the meeting when Mr. Lloyd retired. Also during those years the Young Peoples' Guild began as a result of a campaign in the village. Mr. Raymond Lloyd, came to preach on the evening of Sunday 5th June and no less than eight young people committed their lives to Christ. One of them, Mrs. Glenys Williams (née Jenkins) remembers that night clearly:

> It was in June 1954 that a young preacher, Mr. Raymond Lloyd, came to Zoar Chapel one Sunday and preached on the text, 'There is no difference, for all have sinned and fall short of the glory of God; being justified freely by His grace, through the redemption that is in Christ Jesus' (Romans 3: 22-24). He was a very powerful preacher and so earnest in his zeal to preach the Gospel. God spoke to me in a very clear way that night and

showed me that, although I was a 'good' girl by the world's standards, I was not good enough for God. The preacher made it very clear that we are all sinners before a holy God, and in our own strength we are unable to attain to God's standards. God, in His mercy, made a way back for us through the sacrifices of His Son on Calvary. Only by applying Christ's work to our lives and trusting in His righteousness can we be saved. I realised that I was included in the ALL of Romans 3:23, and that night committed my life to the Lord.

It was as a result of these conversions that Raymond Lloyd returned to Crofty as one of a team led by Mr. John Brayley to hold a campaign in the village. Glenys Williams recalls that Mr. Brayley ran a bicycle and motor bike shop in the Kingsway. Carys Davies, née Ward, was already a Christian at that time and had been instrumental in bringing Raymond Lloyd to Zoar. She writes of the Guild:

We were helped and encouraged by Rev. Lewis Morris, Penuel, teachers and students from the Bible College, Swansea, and Mr. Raymond Lloyd. The Guild was well attended by children of a wide age group, approximately 5-18 years of age. We sang choruses with gusto, read the Bible, prayed, knitted countless squares, which were made into blankets for the less privileged, repaired old hymn books and visited the sick.

During the 1960s the Guild had a visit from Rev. David Davies, now of Waunarlwydd, home on furlough from the Congo where he and his wife, Anne, had been serving with the W.E.C. (Worldwide Evangelization Crusade). Following this visit the young people sent three parcels of clothing out to the Congo, and eventually two bicycles. Many other charities were supported over the years and Mrs. Susan Govier, née Jones, remembers bundling up and selling firewood to raise money for some good cause. Both this children's meeting and the weeknight meeting have continued with hardly a break to the present day.

Zoar Sunday School, winners of the Scripture Examination Cup, 1973.

In 1971 Rev. Ivan Malyon came to Crofty to hold a week of meetings. He was from the Open air Mission. He spoke to gatherings of children and separate meetings for adults on a number of evenings during the week. Mr. Malyon visited some of the members who could not attend because of age or ill health. In 1973 he and his wife, Rita, and the family spent a week's holiday in Crofty when he preached at the Easter services. He subsequently visited the church as a representative of the Society for the Distribution of Hebrew Scriptures.

One of the great strengths of Zoar has been its ability not only to survive but to prosper during its many pastorless years. Another characteristic feature has been the spirit of unity prevailing not only within the church but with the other nonconformist churches in the area. Thirty-two more years without a minister were to pass before the induction of Rev. Meirion Thomas in 1979 as minister of Zoar, Tabernacle and Bethel, Gowerton. He remained until 1983.

In the following year Zoar celebrated the centenary of the church with a whole week of meetings. The preachers on various evenings included Rev. Dafydd Owen, Rev. Bill Steed, Rev. B. Tudor Lloyd and Rev. Russell Williams. On the Tuesday, after tea in the Chapel, Mr. John Fry spoke to the children, who were presented with commemorative plaques inscribed with the verse, 'Remember thy Creator in the days of thy youth' (Ecc. 12:1). On the Thursday, tea was served in Llanmorlais Hall between the services held in the Chapel.

After the departure of Rev. Meirion Thomas, there was a much shorter break before the induction of Rev. B. Tudor Lloyd in 1985, bringing Zoar into the Gower Pastorate to join Burry Green, Cheriton and Old Walls. Mr. Lloyd was already well-known to members of Crofty, having helped with weddings and baptisms for many years while Zoar was without a minister. Crofty fitted easily and amicably into the existing Pastorate which has continued under the ministry of Rev. Iain B. Hodgins since 1995.

8. Music in the Pastorate

Music and singing have always played an important part in the Gower Pastorate. As early as 1875 one of the topics discussed at length by the Gower District Meeting had been how to improve congregational singing. Music has been a unifying factor between the various churches which, although different in background and situation still work well together. An early example is that while Rev. Clement Evans was minister at Penuel in 1896, the chapel in conjunction with Old Walls, Burry Green, Llangennith and Cheriton first held a Music Festival in Old Walls. Later, in 1909, Penuel joined the Singing Festival held annually at Tabernacle. Rev. J. Badham, minister from 1904 until 1910, was one of the founders of the Gower Singing Festival and was its first secretary. William Williams, a faithful deacon at Penuel was chairman of the Festival Committee for many years.

Music has been important in Tabernacle right up to the present day. Rev. William Williams who was minister from 1844 to 1851 wrote of Pen-clawdd: "the Sunday School is fairly successful here, and of the many who attend, most of them show a desire to learn. This success is mainly due to the practice of holding meetings to learn 'pynciau', singing etc., on certain evenings during the week." In those early days music lovers could also attend local eisteddfodau, one of which was held at Tabernacle on Whit Monday in 1869.

When Rev. H. P. James became minister in 1883 he held a weekly singing school for children, to teach hymns and tunes from *Sankey's Sacred Songs and Solos*. From this children's choir developed the Tabernacle Chapel Choir which, under the direction of Mr. J. P. Davies, began to perform easy cantatas and to compete successfully in local eisteddfodau. With Mr. Daniel Jenkins as conductor this choir progressed from cantatas to perform Handel's oratorio *Judas Maccabeus* in 1900, followed by the *Messiah* in the following year. With the exception of the war years, this choir, now known as Côr Pen-clawdd, has performed an oratorio every year in Tabernacle and in Bethel in alternate years.

As far back as 1897 the Church decided to join the Pontarddulais Gymanfa Ganu and by doing so learned a large number of new tunes which proved a great impetus to the hymn singing of the church. Those who had experienced this Welsh Singing Festival thought it would be good to have an English one. Consequently, after a Sunday morning service at Penuel Chapel in the winter of 1908, a meeting was convened by the precentor, the late William Williams, Llanmorlais, to discuss the holding of a Gower Musical Festival. The idea was enthusiastically and unanimously approved, so a committee was formed with William Williams as chairman; the late John Williams, Llanmorlais, as treasurer; and the Rev. J. Badham as secretary. The participants were to be the Calvinistic Methodist churches of Gower, together with 'Gorseinon', referring to Tabernacle, in the same denomination. For the first Festival, held on Whit-Monday, May 31st 1909, Mr William

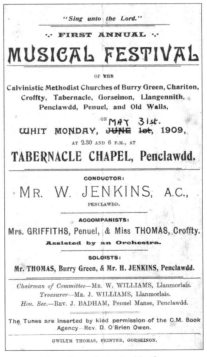

First Annual Festival leaflet.

Jenkins, Penlan, was appointed conductor, Mrs. Phillip Griffiths, and Mrs. Thomas Jenkins, Llanmorlais, were the accompanists "assisted by an orchestra", with "Mr. Thomas of Burry Green and Mr. H. Jenkins, Penclawdd" as soloists. According to the few records that are available, Miss Bessie Dunne of Old Walls acted as co-accompanist with Mrs. Tom Jenkins for a number of years until the new organ was installed in the rebuilt Church of Tabernacle, Pen-clawdd. The Gower Music Festival has been held annually on Whit Tuesday ever since. In addition to this, the Band of Hope children's choir gave performances of many well-known operettas over the years.

In Crofty too, children learnt to sing at an early age from *Sankey's*, and were encouraged to take part in quarterly schools and eisteddfodau. For many years the latter were held annually in Zoar on Christmas night. After the Second World War the chapel choir was re-formed and from 1946 until 1955 gave annual concerts, presenting well remembered cantatas such as *Esther the Beautiful Queen* and *Belshazzar's Feast*.

Although Tabernacle remained in the Welsh Presbytery and did not become part of the Gower Pastorate until 1990, there had been strong links with the Gower churches since the days of Rev. William Griffiths and people from these churches were a part of the Singing Festival from the very beginning, practising the hymn tunes and travelling up to Pen-clawdd for the Festival day. Mr. Deane Gordon of Burry Green was born in 1910 and was taken to the Festival from the age of about six, travelling up to Pen-clawdd for the day on the old Vanguard Bus. It would be jam-packed with people, two rows sitting back to back out on the top, and singing all the way, mostly hymns! At Llanrhidian Cross, it was all out to walk down the hill, as the bus "wasn't too reliable"; it would meet them down on the flat where they all clambered aboard again for the drive along the Marsh Road, depending on the tide. Coming back it would be the same in reverse, this time walking up the hill as the bus couldn't manage that either. It was a great asset, Deane says, when the new road was built. At that time, he remembers, Old Walls folk still travelled up in a horse-brake.

Services were held during the afternoon and evening only, and the children's meeting began just before the war. Tea was served in Tabernacle Schoolroom after the service, strictly limited to those who had bought tea-tickets from a man with a roll of tickets sitting at a table on the path alongside the chapel, leading to the schoolroom door. It was at these teas, seated at the long tables, that Deane learned his first words of Welsh. The tea was poured at the other end of the room and brought round and for some reason, there would be cries of "dim siwgr" [no sugar] all around him. On one occasion one of his uncles took him for a walk after tea and when they came back they were too late to get into the chapel and had to wait until more chairs had been placed down the aisles. All these people came from the Gower chapels, including Penuel, which were then "as strong as Crofty is today". Deane's mind goes back to the times when the big seat was packed full of ministers alone, one from every chapel represented, and some in retirement, returning for the day. The hymns, he remembers, were all taken from the *Church Hymnary* or *Sankey*, and 95% English as Tabernacle was the only church that belonged to the Welsh Presbytery. Each church would submit so many, with the idea of learning new ones from one another. Rehearsals were held, and the one in Burry Green was a big night with three or four horse-brakes coming down from Pen-clawdd, singing all the way. A good number of people sat in the gallery to watch and listen, and refreshments were served before they went home.

In the early days the choir had to learn all its music without the aid of an instrument, and on the occasion of a concert or a competition a piano was hired and the district searched for someone who could play it, however incompetently. When the anniversary services were held, a special effort was made to borrow an American organ, from a church member generally, and it was an amusing sight to see on a Saturday evening half a dozen young men bearing an organ on their shoulders to the chapel in readiness for the next day.

After the very contentious question of whether an organ was appropriate for public worship had been settled, a new reed organ was bought for Tabernacle about the year 1894 and Mr. William Jenkins was appointed organist to both church and choir. With the building of the new chapel in 1911 a new pipe organ was installed by Messrs. Norman and Beard, London, the plans and specifications having been drawn up by Mr. E. T. Davies and the organist.

One of the earliest Precentors was Mr. Robert Clarke, whose strong voice could defy the power of any organ. He was followed by Mr. William Jenkins, Penlan and Mr. David Jenkins. They were succeeded in turn by Mr. Daniel Jenkins and Mr. Ivor Jenkins. A constant reminder of the importance of music in Tabernacle is the unique red Tabernacle hymn book, produced and printed by the church in 1928 and containing hymns in both English and Welsh.

7. 'To rebuild the house'

Iain B. Hodgins

*'Remember your leaders who have spoken the word of God to you.
Consider the outcome of their way of life and imitate their faith.
Jesus Christ is the same, yesterday, today and forever.'*
Hebrews 13:7-8.

The five Presbyterian churches of Gower value the heritage they have entered into, which began with Lady Barham nearly two hundred years ago and has continued through their well-known and less well-known ministers until today. Each generation has produced its lay leaders too, beginning with William Voss who gathered people together in his home, a tradition that continues still with meetings like *Open Home, Open Bible*.

Those who drive past the five church buildings on the way to the surf or the coastal beauty spots could be in no doubt that they are well looked after, although Health and Safety Legislation along with Child Protection Policies have compelled all churches to face up to issues over the care of property and people, issues that earlier generations hardly thought about. Church statistics and policy makers looking at the area might quickly surmise that five churches of the same denomination within a radius of ten miles are no longer necessary, and are even a waste of resources. It will be increasingly necessary for each church to show in future that it is confident of its purpose and calling to serve the community in which it is set.

Christians today face many social and moral questions, just as Lady Barham and William Griffiths did in their time. It is encouraging to see how some of today's members are ready to tackle their civic representatives about such matters, and also to raise pertinent matters in the Courts of the Church.

Sadly, the generations of families who have been the backbone of the five churches for so many years are declining. Most newcomers to the area no longer make affiliation with a church a priority after their arrival. These are days when services are less well attended, and Sunday Schools are not exempt from this trend. Weekday clubs for children, and *Alpha* and *Christianity Explored* courses have been organised recently with the intention of engaging with those who have become lost to the Church.

F. R. Barry rightly assessed the mood of his time when he wrote 'people today do not greatly care about secondary questions of Church order, or the debates of ecclesiastical politics'. Whether his estimation that 'they want to know what is right and what is wrong, who God is and how we can believe in Him', is as true today is debatable. Whatever the answer is, churches need to remember that, 'the purpose of the Church is to worship God and spread the Gospel of the Lord Jesus Christ as it is revealed in the Holy Scriptures and expounded in the Doctrinal standards of the Church, through establishing and maintaining fellowships of people worshipping God and believing in the Lord Jesus Christ' (*Book of Order and Rules of the Presbyterian Church of Wales*, 1978).

In a day of 'small things' it is easy to become satisfied with the mediocre, anticipate gradual decline, and to forget that the church is meant to be more than a holy huddle. There is a need to pray for more people to become disciples of Jesus Christ, with more children and young people being nurtured in the Christian faith, and that each local community should be transformed by the values of God's Kingdom. A suitable prayer might be one that the Diocese of Lichfield has prepared in recent years for its parishioners:

God our Creator and Redeemer,
Help your Church to grow in holiness, unity, effectiveness and numbers.
Draw us closer to you and to those around us.
Give us enthusiasm in our faith,
and wisdom in sharing it with young and old.
Open our eyes to new opportunities,
Our lips to sing and speak of you,
and our hearts to welcome the stranger.

Grow your Kingdom in us and in the world,
through the intercession of our Lord Jesus Christ
and in the power of the Holy Spirit.

Amen.

An answer to that prayer may see many beloved *shibboleths* cast aside, as people come to services informally dressed, to sing twenty-first century hymns, and to sit on soft chairs as they listen to a sermon delivered from a lectern.

It is a contemporary hymn-writer, Christopher Idle, who writes:

Enjoy this meeting place,
And do not count it strange
If God, who gives unchanging grace,
Requires His church to change.

In a changing Church scene, it is clear that the Word of the un-changing God, coupled with the invitation to discover 'life in all its fullness' through His beloved Son is the only message that will draw people together to these *Pleasant Places.*

Professor Francis Lyall, writing in *Serving the Word of God*, which was published in 2002 to celebrate the Rev. James Philip's significant ministry in Edinburgh that began in 1958, says "our hope for the future, lies with ministries similar to those of James Philip, George Philip and William Still. That the preaching of the Word and faithful-ness in prayer should be the keystones, has been demonstrated in those ministries. Other ministries which basically are unqualified social work activity, or divert into political involvement, and congregations which essentially are *fora* for social engagement and nothing else, have no foundation that will last."

Nothing would give the one in whose honour these chapters were written greater pleasure than to hear a fresh generation of people singing with Isaac Watts:

'Come let us seek our God today!'
Yes, with a cheerful zeal
we haste to Zion's hill,
and there our vows and honours pay.

And as members of the five churches, with all true Christian people, we echo what Christopher Idle prays:

Lord God, this house is yours;
May we your people be
Renewed in Christ with all your powers
For Christ eternally.

We do so in the confidence that it is God's will, in this Day of grace, 'that the Lord's house should be built' (Haggai 1:2).

List of Sources

William Griffiths's 'Private Journal, commenced Jany. 1st 1856', in the possession of his great, great grandson, Mr. Peter Griffiths.

[J. Vyrnwy Davies], *A History of Tabernacle C.M. Chapel, Penclawdd, 1836-1936*, Swansea, 1936.

Bethesda Chapel Presbyterian Church of Wales Burry Green 1813-1963, Swansea, 1963.

Zoar, Crofty Centenary Booklet 1884-1984.

Arnold A. Dallimore, *George Whitefield*, Volume 1, London, 1970; Volume 2, Edinburgh, 1980.

Eifion Evans, *A Presbyterian Album: South Pembrokeshire Presbyterian Churches 1913-1999*, South Pembrokeshire Presbytery, 2000.

John Hughes, *Methodistiaeth Cymru*, Tair cyfrol, Gwrecsam, 1851, 1854, 1856.

Alicia Gower Jones, *Gower Memories of William Griffiths*, Aberayron, 1957.

R. Tudur Jones, 'Anghydffurfwyr Cymru 1660-1662', *Y Cofiadur*, 31 (1962), 3-93.

Gerard Noel, *Sir Gerard Noel MP and the Noels of Chipping Camden and Exton*, Campden and District Historical and Archaeological Society, 2004.

Thomas Rees, *History of Protestant Nonconformity in Wales*, Second edition, London, 1883.

T. Rees a J. Thomas, *Hanes Eglwysi Annibynol Cymru*, Cyfrol II, Liverpool, 1872.

Thomas Richards, *Wales Under the Penal Code (1662-1687)*, London, 1925.

Thomas Richards, *A History of the Puritan Movement in Wales*, London, 1920.

Thomas Richards, *Religious Developments in Wales (1654-1662)*, London, 1923.

John Wesley, *Journal*, 8 volumes Standard Edition, edited by Nehemiah Curnock, London, 1909 – 1916.

A. H. Williams, *Welsh Wesleyan Methodism 1800-1858*, Bangor, 1935.

W. Williams, *A Memoir of the Life and Labours of the Rev. Wm. Griffiths, Burry Green, Gower*, London, 1863.

Y Drysorfa, Awst 1859, 274-5: 'Anrheg i'r Parch W. Griffiths, Browyr'.

Y Drysorfa, Gorphenaf, 1862, 241-4: David Howells, 'Y Diweddar Barch. William Griffiths, Browyr'.

Y Cylchgrawn. Calvinistic Methodist Monthly, Swansea and Llanelly, 1851-1870.

Journal of the Historical Society of the Presbyterian Church of Wales, xxxv, 13-18, 'Ymweliad William Griffiths, Browyr, â Llangeitho, 1816', (Miss A. Gower Jones); xlix. 16-21, 'Ymweliad William Griffiths, Browyr, â Sasiwn Abergwaun, 1816', (Miss A. Gower Jones); 21 (1997), 'William Griffiths (1788-1861) – Apostle of Gower', (B. Tudor Lloyd).

Dictionary of Welsh Biography Down to 1940, London, 1959. Davies, David (1763-1816); Ferrar, Robert (died 1555); Griffiths, William (1788-1861); Higgs, Daniel (died 1691); Jones, Griffith (1693-1761); Harris, Howel(l) (1714-1773); Jones, Morgan (mid 17th century); Matthews, Marmaduke (1606-1683?); Miles, John (1621-1683); Rowland, Daniel (1713-1790); Williams, William (1717-1791).

Oxford Dictionary of National Biography: Ferrar, Robert (died 1555); Harris, Howel (1714-1773); Jones, Griffith (*bap.* 1684, *d.* 1761); Miles, John (1620/21-1683); Noel, Diana (1762-1823); Rowland, Daniel (1711?-1790); Williams, William (1717-1791).

The Blackwell Dictionary of Evangelical Biography 1730-1860: Barham, Baroness (1762-1823); Davies, David (1763-1816); Griffiths, William (1788-1861).

Gower

Vol. 10 (1957), 16-18, Gomer M. Roberts, 'Early Methodism in Gower'.

Vol. 52 (2001), 54-66, Gary Gregor, 'William Griffiths: The Apostle of Gower'.

The Banner of Truth, 80: 21-30 Alan F. Francis, 'William Griffiths: the Apostle of Gower'.

Evangelical Magazine of Wales, October 2001, R. Brian Higham, 'Gower'.

The Carmarthenshire Antiquary, xxxvii (2001), 21-30, Glanmor Williams, 'Stephen Hughes (1622-1688): 'Apostol Sir Gâr'; 'The Apostle of Carmarthenshire'.

Appendix 1: William Griffiths (1788-1861), Apostle of Gower

B. Tudor Lloyd

Hyam Maccoby, the Jewish scholar, speaking of the High Priest in New Testament times, says "It was very hard for Gentiles . . . to understand that the religious official who wore the gorgeous robes and presided at religious ceremonies with pomp and circumstance was ultimately of no religious significance, and that the religious authority whom the Jews most revered might be some penurious village shoemaker who was the chief repository of the Law."

The parents of William Griffiths were not penurious shoemakers but smallholders, and they too, because of their piety and religious knowledge, were highly respected as leaders and instructors in religion in the locality of Bwlch-y-groes, Pembrokeshire. Six of their children survived to maturity, and had been given a thorough grounding in Christian faith and morals, not only in chapel but also in their home. William Griffiths had a brother and sister older than he, and three sisters younger. They were deprived of both their parents when he was sixteen years old. "It was a great loss to us their children and loss to the cause of religion in that neighbourhood when they both were removed suddenly in the midst of their usefulness; yet the Lord, who is always infinitely wise and unchangeably good in all that he does, overruled this event for good in the end. His divine care over us fatherless and motherless children was indeed great at that time. We were all young, left to struggle in the world as well as we could, but Providence took special care of us, and the many fervent prayers of our godly parents were answered in the course of the years."

He had already left home to work on other farms when he was fourteen, and was beginning to drift away from the practice of prayer and Bible reading, and even from regular public worship, but not from Christian moral standards. For this he was so grateful to his parents, whose prayers for their children had been as unfailing as their instruction. Years later in Gower he was to complain, "What a great loss we have in this country for want of moral training in families: children are left to grow up just like their animals."

In 1807, as soon as he was 19 years of age, he was balloted into the militia because of the Napoleonic threat, and marched off from Carmarthen with 300 other recruits to join the Carmarthenshire Fusiliers then based in Plymouth Dock. When the regiment was in Bristol, detachments would serve a few months at a time in Milford Haven, and while there, he was visited in the barrack room by his brother, by then a convinced Christian, and later to become an Independent minister much used by God. He brought news of a powerful revival, and deplored his brother's hard lot in ungodly surroundings. In fact, William Griffiths's lot in the army was better than he had expected. He was amiable and uncomplaining, with a good sense of innocent humour, and the old hands were kind to him. Indeed, he was something of a favourite with them.

While marching back to Bristol, he obtained a two-day pass to visit his family 15 miles to the north, and this visit was of great import. Instead of asking him about his army experience in the big wide world, all were telling him of the revival and its effect on them and on the community. No wonder: on one occasion, the chapel congregation divided itself into two groups, one joyful and praising, the other paralysed with awe, with an empty space between them. Now and again, someone with a new and joyous sense of God's love and pardon would leave the silent group to join in the praise and worship of the other. It was this revival which led to the rebuilding and enlarging of Bwlch-y-groes Chapel in 1813.

When it was time to catch up with the regiment, it was his godly eldest sister who rode with him. She spoke of good things and of their parents in heaven, all the way to the outskirts of Carmarthen. She wept much as she turned the horses for home, and once she was out of sight, so did he. He felt that his parents' prayers had been answered in the conversion of their other children, while he was like some 'doomed blackbird'.

For the next two or three days, he was unusually silent and pensive as he marched, and his comrades guessed the reason, calling out, "He's mixed somewhere on Sunday with the Methodists." Because of their teasing, and his shame at being thought religious, by the time they reached Bristol he was to all appearances his usual self, but there was now a new direction to his life. He attended the Welsh Chapel in Broadmead faithfully, stealing away on weeknights as well as on Sunday, and associating with committed Christian men serving in other companies, whom he had hitherto avoided. They became his instructors in "religion of the heart", and he theirs "as far as reading went." When he was very ill with fever, they rallied round him in hospital, and encouraged him in every way to join the Church of Christ. This he decided to do as he stood in his sentry box guarding French prisoners of war in Stapleton Prison. The words came to his mind, "Whoever is ashamed of me and of my words, of him also shall the Son of Man be ashamed when he comes in his glory." He was accepted as a member on the unanimous vote of the congregation, and thereafter he made no secret of his Christian commitment. When his son became a church member, his advice to him was, "Never attempt to hide your profession of religion in any place or company. There is no need of parading our religion before the world by boastful talkativeness; this is Pharisaical vanity: and on the other hand we must not shrink from avowing our adherence to Christ and His cause when the infidel world attempts to frighten us with their jeers, or shame us with their laughter." One lesson he had learnt in the army was to stand by his colours. Another was to value Christian fellowship. Wherever they went, the believers in the regiment found somewhere to meet as a "sincere, united little society", and whenever possible, a chapel to join.

After quelling a riot among the miners one Sunday in Durham, where they had been rushed from Sunderland, in the evening he and his friends were in the Independent Chapel where a distant relative of his father's was minister. "After all the bustle of the day, I found myself very happy in his congregation listening to his sweet instructive sermon on: 'Him that overcometh I will make a pillar in the temple of my God.'" While they were in the area, this minister would travel to preach and conduct 'societies' for them.

When his service in the militia was drawing to a close, the regiment was stationed in Manchester. There he met Rees Jones, a preacher from Anglesey, later to become a lifelong friend. "It was there also I had the privilege of first knowing that great and good man, the Rev. John Elias. He was so concerned about my journeying home through North Wales that he drew up a paper of recommendation to his religious friends on my route home, stating who I was, and requesting them to give me a night's lodging on the way. This added greatly to my comfort, and gave me many new friends. Mr. Elias was also travelling part of my road for several days on his way to Bala. He would always introduce me to the Brethren and send me, though in my red coat, to the pulpit to begin the meetings before the large multitudes who crowded everywhere to hear him."

When he came home, his brother who had been "teaching an English school for some years" gave way to him. William Griffiths had received hardly any schooling since the age of eight, apart from Sunday School, and this gave him the opportunity to further his own education as he taught others. In his opinion, he had "no knowledge of the rules concerning capitals, or of sentences how to form them." As a teacher, he could now also attend evening religious meetings, and catechise Welsh evening and Sabbath schools, something he did a great deal of in Gower. This work was a delight, and in this way, he started to speak in public. What happened next was typical of the Calvinistic Methodist 'Societies' of his day – godly talent spotting. "The religious friends pressed upon me the subject of preaching very earnestly, and though I was unwilling to disclose my feelings, fearing that the Lord had not called me to the work, yet it was very often like fire in my bones and made me fervent in secret prayer for Divine guidance what to do. I was more than a year in this uneasy state." It was not his view, as an Anglican lecturer once put it to a shocked audience of Church of Scotland chaplains, "After all, preaching is just chaps talking."

When a preacher failed to keep an appointment, he volunteered to step into the breach, speaking on a whole psalm. This was the beginning of regular preaching, and soon he was recognized as a preacher within his own Monthly Meeting area.

In October 1816, the Association in Fishguard recognized him as a preacher within the Connexion. This was no formality, and on the night before being examined on his doctrine and religious experience, he dreamt that he was facing a battalion of soldiers all with their muskets aimed and ready to fire. It was this Association which received a request from Lady Barham for help in her evangelistic work in Pen-clawdd, Gower. She sought someone to teach school and preach. Rees Jones had been sent to Pen-clawdd in response to an earlier request from her, and at his suggestion the leaders now asked William Griffiths to go. He agreed to consider the request overnight. If he did not say anything when the matter was discussed in the morning, they would know he was agreeable. He was a shy person, and the less attention drawn to himself the better. His mind was in turmoil, and he had little rest that night. "I sought to lay my whole complaint before the Lord in this matter, and I felt in the morning a strong tendency within me to go, considering in balancing one thing against another that the Lord had an evident call for me to go."

This decision meant disappointment for his dear friends in Pembrokeshire, and upheaval and expense for him, but on January 6, 1817, he set out for Gower in the company of his brother. "The next three days I travelled towards Glamorganshire, and preached twice a day and found the Lord was with me in some degree in most places, particularly at Kidwelly and Llanelli. O that I may be enabled to live to his praise." In those days of spiritual renewal, Calvinistic Methodist preachers saw every long journey as an opportunity to preach along the way, and every group of believers saw in a travelling preacher an opportunity to hear and enjoy the Word of God. The same has applied in Mizoram in recent times. Dr. Biakmawia of Durtlang Hospital told me that when touring the village clinics, he was expected to preach – at length – every evening.

Within a few miles of Pen-clawdd, William Griffiths and his brother were met by Rees Jones with news he could hardly bring himself to speak. Lady Barham had changed her mind, and intended to continue with the Countess of Huntingdon's Connexion rather than depend on the Welsh Calvinistic Methodists. It was the Countess of

...wansea, the godly and much loved Rev. ...ntroduced Lady Barham to Gower in the first ... with the needs of the area. Lady Barham's ...erited shortly before her first visit to Gower ...the Admiralty in the period leading up to the ...nd his wife belonged to the same circle as the ...n, Hannah More and Wilberforce. It was in ...irt, Teston near Maidstone, that the campaign ...ned. When Lady Barham was converted 'late ...t she should look to the Countess of Hunting-...nisters to supply her chapel in Burry Green, ...Gower. They resided a couple of months at a time in the furnished "Chapel House" attached. Rees Jones thought that these English ministers "enraged against us as a body," and were responsible for her change of policy, though the reason Lady Barham gave was a reduction in her financial resources. It seemed that William Griffiths would have to leave the work almost before he had begun. "All these things damped my spirit to some degree, and as I have thought of some Trials, it appeared that now they begin. I felt a little reliance on the Lord, and calmness of mind, always thinking he has some ends to carry on in all these things, as I had no hand at all in it from the beginning till here. But have acted and obeyed in all things the Counsels and Commands of the Association. But through it all it is likely that I was too sanguine for it, therefore it pleased the Lord to put a Bar on my way and call me to listen to him. O that I may understand and be wise – I am now in much darkness respecting Temporals – but not altogether in Spirituals. Blessed be his name, now and then I find a little Liberty in pouring my complaint before him, and some times am enabled to believe that all this will turn for good some way or other which I cannot see at present." This reaction shows his practical Calvinism, and he was right in thinking that all would "turn for good." He lived and ministered fruitfully in Gower until his death, after a few weeks of illness, on July 21, 1861, forty-four and a half years later.

What were the reasons for the clash between the English and Welsh ministers? Their beliefs would be very similar, virtually those of the Church of England apart from differences concerning the three-fold ministry of Bishop, Priest and Deacon.

There was a difference of ethos, and probably of class. The former were college trained, and had a more sophisticated vocabulary. When William Griffiths heard a Mr. Findlay preach in Pen-clawdd, he "did not understand one half of what he said." In 1834, loath as he was to "expect too much from beginners", William Griffiths thought that the chief fault of a student from Carmarthen College was that he spoke in "fine and lofty language to a poor rustic people, who did not and could not understand him." Apart from private reading, the Calvinistic Methodist preachers received 'in service training' through their attendance at Monthly Meetings and Associations, which were more for preaching (starting at 6 a.m.) and theological discussion, than administration. In the early years of William Griffiths's ministry they were virtually revival meetings. Listening to a sermon at a Llangeitho Association in 1816 were "many thousands of all sorts of people, with a lovely expression (*agweddau hyfryd*) on thousands of them." A young man hoping to become a missionary appeals for prayer, and William Griffiths "cannot say how many hundreds were weeping at the same time." All this was ministerial training, but practical and experimental, not academic, just as medical students learnt their skills not so much in classrooms, as in the company of established physicians and surgeons. The Association 'society' meetings could be deemed seminars, as for example in Neath in 1820. "Had the best part of the society in which I saw much of the Lord's presence with his ministers helping them to search for truth and wisdom – giving them much humility and liberality of mind and all full of harmony." Harmony was very important to him in the local and denominational setting. In his early days as a preacher in Bwlch-y-groes, he had gone on a preaching tour, and found on his return that there had been a rift in the church. His distress was great, and he could not rest or cease from prayer until there was unity again. Two women in Burry Green are threatened with discipline unless they become better friends. No sooner do two farmers fall out over animals trespassing, than they are brought to a reconciliation sealed with a handshake, at the next 'society' – "lest others be drawn in." "I am thankful that we have not been frequently troubled in Gower with contention between church members." Harmony between the Associations in the North and in the South was of prime importance to him. He was, for example, a great supporter of the London Missionary Society, but was distressed that the Calvinistic Methodist Missionary Society was set up before sufficient time had been given to bring the North fully to the same mind on the matter. He saw the dismissal of an early missionary as possibly a sign of Divine displeasure at this imperilling of Connexional unity. It was he and the Rev. R. Humphreys who were sent to London in 1849 to heal the rift in the Jewin Crescent Church. "We were there part of five days and succeeded to the letter of our instructions, and left them in peace as far as outward profession of it – the Lord only knows the heart."

To come back to the English ministers: they used a Book of Common Prayer (probably that in use in the Countess of Huntingdon's Connexion) which William Griffiths, and probably Rees Jones, did not find helpful. William Griffiths grieved to see people "ready to sleep" as the prayers were read. His own 'liberty' of expression, 'access' to God, and holding the people's attention were as important to him in public prayer as in preaching. He made sure people heard him. After his first sermon in the Field Chapel, Spafield, London, where he was supplying the pulpit for six Sundays, the chapel clerk told him that "the congregation are averse to loud preaching", and with characteristic wisdom he took the hint. Probably some of the English ministers of his early days in Gower shared the same aversion as the fashionable London congregation, and this helped to give the impression that they had "high opinions of themselves and prejudice against others." Rees Jones and William Griffiths did not have the polished manners of those who moved in aristocratic circles. John Elias wrote a wise and practical letter to Rees Jones in which he touched on this very topic, advising him on how he should conduct himself when in Fairy Hill, Lady Barham's residence. It was something of a test of the English ministers' humility therefore when the people gave a readier hearing to the home spun young Calvinistic Methodists, than to them. Indeed, in an attempt to safeguard the attendance at Burry Green, the decision was taken to stop William Griffiths preaching on a Sunday evening in Cheriton, where during the week he was teacher, the sole teacher, of as many as 60 or 70 children. (He was expected to be in Burry Green on Sunday mornings and for 'societies'.) Despite his hurt, he decided it was "his wisdom to be silent" and to make it a matter of prayer. To his joy, in a few months he was allowed to resume as before, for which he praised his Heavenly Father.

That William Griffiths was critical of read prayers did not prevent him from appreciating many a "sweet and experimental" and "refreshing" sermon from some of the readers of those prayers. It was the way some of them conducted the society meetings which provoked his greatest criticism. For him, the society was an opportunity for "searching and seeking after the true work of the Holy Spirit on the soul", but at a society in Burry Green he saw "so little" of this, and "so much urging the people to rejoice and to take comfort under the notion that a change had taken place in them – without attending to the present frame of their mind . . . whether fit for such joy and comfort or not. O what different hearts have these English ministers to mine which is still rebellious – hard – full of abominable lusts and all manner of sin. But how can such a worm as me be comfortable until I am brought out of these – how can I come out unless almighty power comes to my aid. And when he in infinite mercy brings me up I believe then with David, 'Although my house is not so with God: yet he hath made with me an everlasting covenant, ordered in all things and sure.' Then am I desirous to acquaint the Lord's people with sweet and good tidings – 'Come, all ye that fear God, hearken to what he hath done for my soul.'" Again, of a Burry Green society meeting he says, "More hurt than benefited – the Lord was pleased to keep me from any angry passions which I have too often felt towards the minister – yet it was manifest enough to me that he encouraged hypocrites to say what they never knew nor felt – and that he discouraged, yea, checked one or two to say what I am persuaded were the exercises of the Spirit on their hearts – under pretence that complaining of our hardness and temptations are by no means fit to be mentioned in Society lest they discourage others, etc. But all should be – the goodness of the Lord towards us, and the pleasure we find in his work – I think that Society is for saying the truth (when anything is asked) whether the former or latter or both may be our experience." (Thirteen years later he takes a possibly different attitude in dealing with a certain 'T.T.', though not in the context of a society. He writes, "There seems to be something about him bordering on melancholy, and he seems to give way to it until he is painful to himself and others . . . advised him not to allow his feelings to rule his outward deportment too much, lest he should hurt others as well as himself.")

The 'English minister' who was slow to probe souls was quick to say that every Christian should be able to say that he is 'delivered'. "Another remark staggered me – much damped the poor young man it was addressed to – 'unless we can say of the Lord's *deliverance* of our souls by the Blood of Christ we know nothing of true religion' – without this I truly believe we cannot have true religion – and believe as firmly that many have it who cannot, yea dare not say, what they *have* till such time as the Lord is pleased to enable them." Now William Griffiths was a person of undoubted spiritual experience and joyful appreciation of the Gospel and its privileges. He wrote for example, "Had sweet liberty in private prayer . . . saw some wonderful glory in the Person of Christ, and the privilege of poor guilty sinners – a right as such to come to him. O Blessed Saviour, and Blessed, ever Blessed salvation – full and free for the guilty". Yet his attitude for most of his ministry was this: "I would not deliberately say for anything, that I am not born again, yet I cannot say that I am." J. J. Morgan writes that following rich blessings during the 1859 Revival, William Griffiths asked an old lady in a society meeting, "Do you enjoy the society?" "Yes," she said, "otherwise I would not have kept coming to them for over fifty years." "Is your pack ready yet?" "No, it isn't." "It should be." "Is your pack ready, Mr. Griffiths?" "Yes." "Since when?" "Five years ago" (i.e. after forty years of preaching). "Indeed," said the old lady, "if I were you, I'd open that pack again, in case you've forgotten something." William Griffiths had packed and repacked his faith and experience every birthday, every New Year, every Communion Service, and many, many other times. "Am often full of fears in regard to the state of my soul before God, yet I am more full of fears that the Lord will permit sin to break out and bring an open reproach upon his Gospel." His longing for holiness was very real and very necessary. No Christian can evade the command, 'Be ye holy, for I am holy.' But his underlining in the following quotation may show, at least at the time of writing, that his understanding of the place of personal holiness in the Christian life is inconsistent with its place in the doctrine of justification by faith: "it is holiness that effectually and finally saves the soul; it is holiness I love, and holiness I desire – yet I find more unholiness in myself every day ready to manifest itself in some way or other." This sense of indwelling sin he allows to cast doubt on his conversion. What he has always known as a doctrine, "not my changes, but his own faithfulness is the standard of my salvation," he fails to apply for his comfort. He begins to see this in Jan. 1851, "I dwelt too much and too long with my inward man for proof of sincerity, the heart always being wicked and deceitful as the home of the old man – look to Jesus, O my soul." His advice to himself reminds us of Staupitz's life-giving advice to Luther, "to see his election in the wounds of Christ," not in his own troubled soul. After reading so many of William Griffiths's soul searchings, it is a relief to remember a scholar's comment, "For the Roman Catholic, assurance of salvation is presumption: for the Puritan (and William Griffiths was designated affectionately more than once as 'the old Puritan') it was a privilege; for the New Testament believer, it was simply a fact."

William Griffiths had come to Gower as a teacher and preacher, at first to help Rees Jones. This he was allowed to do for a few months as an act of grace on Lady Barham's part. He was then appointed to take the place temporarily of the sick teacher of the school in Cheriton. Sadly, the pious young Philip Gwyn did not recover, but became yet another Gower victim of tuberculosis, brought about so often by poverty and living in overcrowded cottages.

William Griffiths's assessment of the importance of teaching may be judged by the fact that every day he prayed for strength to speak to the children. He was a disciplinarian, but had the affection of his pupils, and was proud of their behaviour and deportment, e.g. at 'school inspections' or, too often, at the graveside of classmates. When, after three years and eight months, he was moved away to start another school and church in Pilton Green, some eight miles to the south, his last day as their teacher ended like this. "Their [the children's] tears in the evening were too much for my feelings to look them in the face – nor to proceed with my exhortation." While he was in Pilton Green, Lady Barham changed her allegiance to the Independents, because the Calvinistic Methodists would not agree to her request that her secretary, William Hammerton, be ordained. Hammerton had not gone through the usual Calvinistic Methodist procedures. Even though his brother by this time was a minister with the Independents, William Griffiths's loyalty to his beloved Connexion was unswerving. In three years or so, in a letter to his wife-to-be, he refers to the Connexion as: ". . . the distinguished connexion in which we have the privilege of being members; distinguished by God in regard to piety, purity of doctrine and discipline, sympathy and good sense, from any other community in the whole world, according to the testimony of many excellent people who are not members in it." This uncompromising allegiance led ultimately to his dismissal, the precursor of which was Lady Barham's unprecedented refusal to allow him to attend an Association. "I kept school till middle day, and then dismissed the children as the other schoolmaster did not come to take it off my hands. The piercing cries of the dear little children as they stood up to go away, so overpowered my feelings that I was not able to speak a word, and had nothing to do but withdraw and leave them. I heard their cries at a long distance from the chapel. I thought I would suffer any hardship to remain with them, and keep my place in the chapel: but that is all over now . . . I must make up my mind to remain in Gower. I cannot leave the work which I have begun, nor quit the field, because others will not allow me to join them. O Lord, send now prosperity."

The Association agreed that a Calvinistic Methodist cause be established in Gower, with the proviso that 'no just cause of offence' be given to Lady Barham's Connexion. An abandoned Wesleyan Chapel in Old Walls was renovated as the C.M. Chapel, a Preaching

Room was fitted out in Overton, with 12 preaching stations established in private houses. Then followed the most laborious toil of his busy life as, on foot, he maintained a constant round of preaching. Hitherto, for longer journeys, he had often enjoyed the loan of a horse from Lady Barham's stable.

Then came a startling development – after two years, Lord Barham, who had inherited Burry Green and Cheriton Chapels, seeing them deserted, asked him to be the resident minister under his patronage in Burry Green. He accepted the post, which he never sought, only on condition that it was fully understood that he was a minister of the Welsh Calvinistic Methodists, and subject to their discipline and procedures. The next crisis came twelve years later when Lord Barham withdrew his patronage, and it was rumoured that Burry Green Chapel (Bethesda) was to become an Anglican Chapel of Ease. The reason for this change was that the Rector of Reynoldston, Parson Phillips, had married Lord Barham's sister. However, apart from the loss of stipend, his ministry continued as before. In 1855, at William Griffith's request, Lord Barham, now the Earl of Gains-borough, donated the chapels and manse to the Calvinistic Methodists. Throughout their lives, the two men held each other in mutual respect, and exchanged letters. William Griffiths, as he read over his journals of years before, never ceased to marvel at God's goodness to him when all had looked so dark, and all he could do was trust and pray.

William Griffiths was gifted as a preacher as well as teacher. So much so, that within months of his coming to Gower, Lady Barham suggested that she should let Rees Jones go, and make him her minister in Pen-clawdd. He declined without hesitation, but the offer is a testi-mony to his preaching abilities. What made him a good preacher?

He had a definite conception of what a good sermon should be, and we can tell this from his assessment of other people's sermons. An Association sermon delivered by John Thomas, Cardigan, was "cutting like a sword and sweet as honey to my soul. I was glad to be here and wished to be here continually." A curate's sermon in Llanmadoc was "pointed and searching and consistent with scripture – well adapted to the state of his hearers." On the other hand, another's sermon is "full of nourishing morality", but he obviously feels that merely telling people to be good is not going to have much effect. Hoping he is not being prejudiced, he comments after hearing a Wesleyan local preacher, "I wished to see more concern for the glory of God and a greater sense of human depravity – O that all who engage as public teachers were to feel more of the power of religion in their own souls, before they undertake the sacred office. *I found nothing in this harangue calculated to instruct the understanding or to impress the conscience* ." He can be critical of the congregation too: "These people praise everything as good and wonderful – when very few among them all have any judgment to discern good from bad." Of another occasion he writes, "Not able to make anything of the sermon – persuaded that a hundred years of such preaching would produce no saving effects." In his own preaching, he looked for the effect of his words on the faces of the people; not for him a fixed gaze at his notes, or an unfocussed stare over the people's heads. "I was like a man shooting arrows against hard rock which were flying back again to my face – except a little few that seemed otherwise – O when will the time come in these poor, ignorant, proud souls to change their hearts and manners." Spurgeon speaks of some preachers who get through a lot of ammunition in the pulpit, but make sure that none of the congregation gets hit: that stricture certainly would not apply to William Griffiths.

He was determined to communicate, whether by spoken or written word. He did this equally well in Welsh and English, and had applied himself early to achieve this rare ability. As soon as he knew he would need to preach in English, he began keeping his journal in English, and soon set about preparing his sermons, even the ones he would preach in Welsh, in that language. Later, after years of speaking and preaching in English, and feeling Welsh to be the more unfamiliar pulpit language, when he knew he would be travelling through Welsh areas on his annual preaching tour, or was preaching in Tabernacle, Pen-clawdd, where the services had always been conducted bilingually, he reversed the process, and prepared his sermons in Welsh. He knew that once he could express his ideas in the less familiar language, he would have no difficulty in doing so in the other.

Facility of language ensured that he was understood, but he also had to gain and hold attention. After a conversation with friendly non-religious neighbours, he comments, "I have no parts nor zeal to tell to worldly people about religion etc. and that in a way suitable to their state – and at the same time engaging – O Lord, help me in this important point." The help he sought for his preaching, he also sought for his magazine articles. He did not see the point of good sound articles which no-one would read. Knowledge and instruction needed to be clothed in "suitable easy and striking expressions."

He aimed to make his sermons interesting, relevant and full of striking truths. When Burry Green is full of "giddy young people", he introduces his sermon in a "familiar, conversational style", asking them why they thought they were there in the service. "If they came to some great man's house, and were asked what they wanted, they would look very foolish if they had nothing to say. Indeed, the great man might be rather offended. The house they were now in belonged to Someone far, far greater than any owner of an estate. Why had they come? It should be to hear God's message to them. Let them listen to the text of the sermon then. 'Today, if ye hear His voice, harden not your hearts . . .'" The young people listened with rapt attention and seriousness. Once he preached for an hour and twenty minutes in a house crowded with youngsters. That sermon he thought was "too long for young people," but they gave him their riveted attention throughout.

His texts had to be clear to him, and this could only come about with God's help. "At home in my study all day – had some painful thoughts about my spiritual ignorance, and want of mind and method as a preacher of the Gospel. If I fail in preparing my sermons to reach the heart of my text by original thoughts of my own, with easy connexions and transitions, it is no wonder that I fail in the delivery of them to make impression on the heart of my hearers – I must reach this desirable gift, if ever I shall obtain it, by more frequent and fervent prayer. The Lord is able and willing to give it – but I must not expect any blessing but in the channel which the promise sets before me – that is by obtaining a larger supply of the Holy Ghost as the Spirit of Christ . . . sent to enlighten the mind with ministerial gifts."

He was quick to see spiritual lessons in his everyday experiences, and probably these would be used as sermon illustrations. He comes across a dead animal, with its unbearable stench. That is what he, with all his sin, was like in God's sight, but God in His love had come and embraced him. Old Walls Chapel is severely damaged in a storm: what must the storm of death be to those who are unprepared for it? "O my soul, build on the Rock that can withstand any storm."

An American book on preaching says, "When you stand up to preach, don't think the congregation are sitting on the edge of their pews waiting for you to speak. They are probably rather bored, and have a shrewd suspicion that you are not going to improve matters." William Griffiths's congregations did look to him in eager anticipation, and it caused him pain if he thought he had failed them. "Less freedom this time – low spirit and inward pain in seeing a large congregation going away, fearing I was not instrumental in reaching their hearts." On one occasion it was because he hadn't prepared sufficiently, choosing a text "at a venture. I hope this will teach me in future not to go so little prepared." He knew nevertheless that however well prepared his sermon might be, something far more important was needed, namely the help of God's Spirit to bring home the message, not only to his hearers but to himself. "Lord, I am about to go away for a week to preach to other people – O Lord, water my soul." "I am never satisfied with freedom of words and general matter in preaching, when my heart is not affected – I consider myself in such case as the water wheel that turns the mill, grinding food for others, but nothing for itself." "Let my sermon be ever so full of matter, and ever so well studied, if I am left to myself in preaching it – it is like cold meat without relish – or a rusty sword without edge – the people then appear stupid and careless – the godly portion of them, expecting and anxious, but not satisfied – my own soul in pain – my body in greater exertion and fatigue than usual – my spirits low and unhappy in retiring, and almost ready to give up the work – but when Divine help is given, all is pleasure, and new desires arise for the glory of God and the saving of souls." An entry in his diary in November 1845 is significant: "Low in spirit, but the Lord gave more than usual light and power, though nothing very deep or extraordinary in what I advanced. There was a searching light and power going with it, which made everyone present to fix their eyes and stare in my face, and many to hang down their heads and weep floods of tears."

This coincidence of simple truths with light and power is characteristic of revival. A recent revival in Mizoram was led by an evangelist who had received minimal schooling, but high and low flocked to hear him in their thousands, among them the Chief Minister of Mizoram and the staff of Durtlang hospital (in relays). The Medical Director and his Deputy said that their experience of God through those simple messages left them different men. William Griffiths longed and prayed for revival in Gower throughout his ministry. Whenever he heard of revival elsewhere, his typical prayer is "O that some drops may fall on poor, dry, barren Gower."

In December 1845 there is this significant entry in his diary and an even more significant marginal note. "None of late have manifested a desire to join the cause of the Redeemer – I sow the seed in hope. I often say, 'Lord, what will be the result of the vision of the Gospel, and the preaching of Christ among these people. Behold I have long laboured, with very limited success in the direct conversion of souls to God – the valley appears still full of dry bones and at present very little commotion is seen, but the answer of the Lord is. 'The vision is yet for an appointed time, but at the end it shall speak and not lie; though it tarry, wait for it.' My particular prayer today has been to be more weaned in thoughts and affections from every worldly care and worldly plans, and fixed upon God's faithfulness." The note in the margin says, "It is now fifteen years since this page was written. Now the Vision begins to speak." In that year, he received many new members, mostly young people and young married couples, more than he had ever received before – after "long expectation and much prayer, the Lord had been pleased to hear me, and greatly comforted my soul."

He had experienced revival in other parts of the country, particularly in the Neath and Swansea areas in 1829. Not everything in that revival is to his taste, but he has no doubt that revival is a very great blessing indeed, and is to be defended as such. "I feel sorry to see the subject of the present revival at Neath and the neighbourhood taken up by the newspapers, with so much spleen and indignation, though the writers profess to serve religion, by holding forth the unpardonable excesses of enthusiasm to contempt and ridicule. Excesses there are no doubt, and every wise and pious man laments to see so much noise and confusion in places of worship – yet the Lord works powerfully on the souls of hundreds and the moral effects are excellent – no enemy can deny it . . . so many hundreds of young people, mostly ashamed to be seen among religious people, much more so, to hear their own voice in a place of worship, are affected. In these great excitements many persons of the most abandoned character were truly converted from their sinful courses and lived from that time forth an ornament to religion and a blessing to all their neighbours – and also that the standard of morals has been much higher in such places than it was before – these and many more enquiries of the like nature ought to be made before judging rashly as some spectators of some outward irregularities which no wise or pious man wishes to justify."

He sees the revival at first hand when the services marking the opening of Trinity, Swansea, are combined with those of the Monthly Meeting. Hundreds were turned away and the Welsh Service was interrupted: "– it was all in one sound of praise and jumping – others showing much disapprobation in their countenances – I felt my heart too cold to enjoy the pleasure some of the spectators seemed to feel – those who were shouting, lifting up their hands and jumping were very numerous, and continued for a long time after the service was over – I trust the most part were sincere, and could not refrain from their violent gesticulations – my prayer was, 'O Lord, take care of thy own glory' as I knew many scoffers and prejudiced men were present."

The next day, "at ten and two I never knew anything like . . . I should have liked it much better if they could have showed a little more decency in the worship of God – but I must say nothing lest I should mistake – certainly the ministers this time, one of them in particular, did encourage it – this I consider very improper, knowing how easy it was to move the passions. I hope much good will be done in this New Place – may this memorable day prove the birthday of many sinners." He himself is far from encouraging emotionalism; he knew that blessing from on high could come silently, as happened in a notable Association in Llantwit Major, when Ebenezer Richards and John Elias preached, and "Many seemed to receive the truth with silent ecstasies of joy." He is glad to avoid excitement: "The Lord was pleased to help me in preaching clear and easy without exciting their passions to interrupt me as has frequently been the case since the revival has commenced." His purpose is to establish the converts: "I trust the Lord will bless the subject of this evening to confirm them in the truth." His text was 1 Chron. 12:17, 18, stressing that this was a "covenant engagement." The "everlasting covenant, ordered in all things, and sure" was a favourite theme, "ordered in all things – nothing left out." This truth, highlighted by Calvin, was an anchor to him in all his disappointments and trials. "Blessed covenant, blessed God who made it."

Before he had his own trusty mare, he travelled on foot, or on a borrowed steed when available, sometimes as far as Llansamlet and Penllergaer, some 15 or 17 miles away. One Christmas Day found him attending a Monthly Meeting 30 miles distant in Pyle. On one occasion, he walked with his wife and baby son the last few miles to Llanelli, traversing very boggy ground in the rain. He never forgot the tender care bestowed on his wife and child on that occasion by a Davies family. I suspect that his wife was suffering from post-natal depression, and that is why he was loath to leave her behind. His usual mode of transport was on horse back, but he also made use of coastal shipping – packet boats from Swansea to Bristol, and from Anglesea to Liverpool. He once came back to Gower from Llanelli in a pilot boat.

When minister in Burry Green, he regularly undertook, usually once a year, a preaching tour of four to six weeks, sometimes averaging two sermons a day and not sleeping in the same bed two nights in succession. When travelling, he knew he could not prepare new sermons, and therefore prayed for grace to preach old sermons in a fresh manner. At home, he needed grace to prepare new sermons. He was wary of making impromptu additions to old sermons, in case these would be repeated without being tested adequately in the light of

Scripture as a whole and the analogy of faith. Everything said from the pulpit had to be tested and reliable. He twice occupied Rowland Hill's pulpit in Watton under Edge over a period of six weeks, and on the second visit a gentleman waited on him "to acknowledge the blessing he had received" during the previous visit, when he had been converted. William Griffiths was very impressed with the congregation, embracing as it did people of "all grades in Town and neighbourhood." They were impressed with him too, and hints were dropped about a change of pastorate, but he made it clear that he would not leave Gower, despite a liking "for a settled ministry."

Attending Associations involved preaching along the way, an example of "our present pattern of a galloping string of preaching" – a pattern which he thought had its deficiencies, but nevertheless had brought "a blessing to thousands and tens of thousands in Wales." At least twice he almost lost his life crossing estuary or river, and riding eighteen miles across the Brecon Beacons in pouring rain was not a comfortable experience, nor was travelling in areas where "cholera raged" a safe one: but "being in the path of duty" he did not let these things disturb him.

As he was only the thirty-third Calvinistic Methodist minister to be ordained, he knew the Connexion when it was still a revival movement, and saw it become more of an institution. He warmly welcomed some developments, such as the Aged and Infirm Ministers and Widows Fund. His friend Rees Jones had died leaving a widow and five young children; there was a real need for such provision. When Trefeca College was founded, he undertook special preaching services to help fund it. This he also did to encourage congregations to help themselves and each other to get out of their debt on buildings. Home and foreign mission work called for administration and oversight. All this entailed committee meetings in addition to the regular meetings of the Association. Even in today's less demanding Associations, delegates can sympathise with his comment: "Attended six meetings, two hours each and more – faintings and giddiness in my head. The last committee did not break up until ten at night." Of interest is the change that took place in the Llandovery Association in 1846, "At

8 a.m. the private meeting for ordination was held in the chapel – it was granted this time that pious females who wished might be present, and there was a large number in the gallery." He makes no adverse comment, so evidently he approved. It was his second service of the day, having already preached at the six o'clock service.

He feared that the Connexion was losing something as the years went by. Even before he left Bwlch-y-groes, Ebenezer Richards's unforgettable cry in one Association was, 'Ble mae'r tân?' (Where is the fire?), but powerful sermons like that fanned the flames of spiritual life. William Griffiths was disappointed in some of the leaders who succeeded "our fathers." One in particular seemed to lack humility, and to be dictatorial. He was pleased to see him outvoted on a matter "of a trifling nature. He seemed to feel it so much – perhaps it may be useful for him in future. O how precious is humility – how much this grace is wanted in this present day – O my soul pray for humility and practise the self denial that leads to the mind of Christ." It is typical of William Griffiths that whenever he criticizes someone, he prays for himself. The following observations on his disappointment and forebodings concerning denominational decline, serve as a warning to any ecclesiastical organization. "Pain . . . from the conduct of a certain leading individual – the want of brotherly love and esteem for the opinion of others, was I think, the principal features of selfishness that guided him – much of the meeting was lost in the technicalities about words." "General unction, but nothing of the power very frequent in former years – perhaps the difference is not felt or inquired into as it ought. The truth is now preached full and clear, but where is the fire that frequently fell under the ministry of our former Elijahs? The Lord has not forsaken his people, many things remain that prove his presence, yet he does not attend the word with the same demonstration of Divine power – the multitudes still congregate – good order is observed in the camp – but very probably more thought is spent on the outward than the spiritual part of the work – the Holy Spirit is quenched because not fervently sought."

"The cause just now is in a very lukewarm state and symptoms of yet worse times appear unless some powerful visits from God's Spirit will be given to prevent it. The rising generation of young ministers and leaders (with of course worthy exceptions) are dogmatical in spirit, selfish in opinion, and not very respectful towards hoar hairs; their zeal also appears chiefly in questions of second importance – relative to new theories in practice – more than the anxiety for a deeper tone of piety and hearts devoted to holiness." He speaks of young ministers arguing for arguing's sake, displaying "a spirit of opposition and retaliation. We have plenty of men who are fond of talking and judging, but very few willing to work and suffer for the work of Christ and the Gospel – most seek their own things."

Because of other business intruding, "a precious opportunity of discussing a religious subject which had been intended for this meeting" was lost. "O shall the great adversary have his long wished opening to enter in among us, as he has had in other denominations? Shall this hitherto beautiful field of Gospel cultivation in the moral desert of Wales be laid waste again, and all this well adapted machinery for great usefulness be laid aside because little opinions of little men more carnal than holy, are likely to disturb the harmony of the Connexion?"

He proceeds to liken the denomination to spoilt children living in a false optimism on the work and reputation of their fathers, though indulging in "sloth and selfish applause." "The eyes of the Lord are upon us, seeing our barrenness, our selfish desires, worldly motives, want of love to him and to one another, readiness to find fault with all measures or movements if we are not consulted, or have no particular hand in them – truly we are guilty of all this and more – yet our precious Redeemer will, I hope, spare the Connexion, and in great mercy remove the present painful signs of the times."

He disliked acrimony in debate, disregard for the feelings of others, and misplaced zeal. "I felt truly sorry for several brethren this time; the zeal displayed deserved a better cause than the one defended and gave the enemy an advantage over brethren to inflict wounds that cannot be so easily removed. This is a sad feature that distinguishes the present generation of church officers in our Connexion from the Fathers that are gone – a dogmatic spirit – very little regard for the feelings of others."

This regard for the feelings of others extended to his attitude to other denominations. Though he felt it when some of his flock were lured away – "Our brethren the clergy, who are evangelical, use all their means to draw all who begin to appear serious after them, and are much more bigoted than the other clergy" – he consoles himself with the thought, "Why grieve, if they will be in heaven after serving in another portion of the King's Army?" He himself would not receive anyone from another church without a letter of transfer.

The Wesleyans at first were very prejudiced against him, but before long he received "much favour" from them, "though the leaders are far from being friendly to our doctrine." When the Association in Merthyr agreed to hold preaching services in the various churches of the town, it was the request of the Primitive Methodists that he should be their preacher. It was with reluctance that he had accepted an invitation to attend the Wesleyan Branch Missionary Society in Pilton Green, but was glad afterwards that he went. "It were well if all denominations of Christians were more liberal in their private opinion of one another – this no doubt would open the way for more good to be done in the world, and more individual happiness and spiritual enjoyments in this life – though we cannot and must not expect to see eye to eye in this world, yet we ought to allow others the same freedom of opinion, as we expect from them to think and judge for ourselves – if this sentiment were once felt, and properly understood, amongst all Christians, it would be the means of much good and would destroy the power of prejudice, selfishness and backbiting, and disappoint Satan of his strongest hold, by which he creates discord among the saints."

He knows that he longs to be useful to God and instrumental in the conversion of sinners, but he cannot be sure whether his zeal springs from "the work of faith and love in my soul, or from selfish principles to advance my name and party – one thing I know that when a sinner is converted I feel my heart knit to him in love. I know my predilection to be very strong in favour of the little church in my own care – it is my greatest happiness, next to the salvation of my own soul, to see this prospering – yet I pray daily for a liberal mind, and view the whole church of Christ as one great corporation, having but one head, and one real interest in the world – bigotry is the bane of spiritual prosperity – the prominent and lovely features of real Christianity fade before this cursed spirit and wither away like blighted trees that bring no fruit." In some of these sentiments, consciously or unconsciously, he echoes the very words of John Elias and John Newton.

For thirty and more years he regularly conducted a society in Overton, a society which brought him more times of refreshing than any. Following these visits, he would preach in nearby Port Eynon. Now he is unable to continue travelling there on account of his health, and lack of overnight lodging. He is however happy to think that his erstwhile hearers would be strengthening the Anglican and Wesleyan churches.

While he thought there was unfairness to nonconformists in the prevailing ecclesiastical system, he did not want to see a zealous campaign in favour of disestablishment divide and possibly embitter Christian people. He opposed "Puseyism" as being virtually the same as Roman Catholicism, which he blamed for the persecution of Protestant believers on the mission field and elsewhere. It was not only he who was wary of Romanism. The issue of *Y Drysorfa* which contained the first of his two articles on 'Gwir a Gau Addoliad' (True and False Worship) also had an article on why the Apostle Peter was not the first Pope. One reason given was, 'The Papal Church forbids all its clergy to marry, which is a devilish device to further its worldly influence, and is a source of innumerable evils.'

William Griffiths was not forbidden to marry, but it was some time before he found a much desired helpmeet. In his search he knew sadness and disappointment, but was upheld in his prayerful desire to live worthily of the Gospel in this area of life, as in every other. He proposed to one young lady by letter, handing it over "trembling" as he and Rees Jones, together with a number of young people, made their way to an Association in Llandeilo. Confiding in Rees Jones as the two of them walked to their lodging, he was dismayed to find that his friend too was awaiting a response from the same person to the same proposal! They determined that this should not affect their friendship, and it was Rees Jones who was accepted – but it was a trying time for them and the young lady.

He exchanged notes with someone, 'F. D.', who resided in Fairy Hill, Lady Barham's residence. His prayers at this time are typical of his caution and trust. "O Lord, guide and guard me from the awful rocks upon which many have split in these precarious undertakings." "He *will order all things well* and what he will do [will be] the best for me." It was arranged that he should have a private conversation with her in Bethesda Chapel House, where Lady Barham's minister resided. "This was the first interview of this nature and perhaps the last for ever – as my friend is to leave this country for her native place and there to remain." They parted after William Griffiths read from Isaiah 42 and prayed, and both were "melted to tears". More than six months later he received a letter he did not expect after such a long time from "someone for whom I still feel a tender regard. It enters not on the subject proposed in mine, but promises another if Providence will spare the person to return home. Is now just gone to France – may the Lord keep her soul from the snares of an alluring world and a tempting devil." Lady Barham was of Huguenot extraction, and the Earl of Gainsborough was about to sail for France when he wrote one of his letters to William Griffiths. My guess is that 'F.D.' was one of Lady Barham's younger daughters.

Two years later, William Griffiths wrote another letter proposing marriage to a pious lady who lived just outside Gower, Rachel Morgans. The friend entrusted with the letter did not deliver it. William Griffiths gives the sad reason: "It was that day fortnight that the Lord called her to the eternal world (after a few days sickness in a fever). I was glad to find that my friend never delivered the letter because of her illness, and was even more glad to find that she died triumphant – infinite better marriage than if she had been united to me to share in the toils of this vain world." This leads him to think about Providence, and his need to "rely more upon God – less upon my own wisdom."

Another two years go by, and he writes a letter, delivered by a friend, which begins, "Dear Miss Jones, You will be surprised no doubt when you will open this letter and find it comes from a person almost unknown to you." In a couple of months he sets out to preach in Llandeilo, but with an important visit to make in Talley. On setting out, his prayer is, "O that the Lord may go with me and direct all the proceedings that may result, for his glory and my comfort"; his prayer on returning is Eliezar's, "Blessed be the God of my master Abraham, who hath led me in the right way." In a few months' time, in July 1826, he and Alicia Gratiana Jones are married. He is thirty-six, and his wife about three years older. Their only child William is born to them in 1828.

In one of his letters to his future wife, William Griffiths states that he does not expect Paradise on earth, because "my Directory says, 'In the world ye shall have tribulation' – yet I know I shall by the Divine blessing be more happy than I am now." One of the tribulations they had was William's illness, a swelling in one of his knees, "which was not painful except when treated." As one of the treatments was a perpetual blister, this is not surprising. This kept him from school, and his father fears that this might be making him of a "somewhat indolent nature." Doctors' fees were expensive, but he is grateful that he can meet them without going into debt. The most benefit was received in Llanwrtyd and Llandrindod Wells, thriving spas for many years to come, but the boy's ailment continued at least into young manhood. Another tribulation was William's apprenticeship to a Swansea pharmacist, good at his profession, but a "Pharaoh" of a man. When William went down with small-pox, Mrs. Griffiths nursed him for three weeks in the December cold in an unheated room with only a chair to sleep in.

Never did William Griffiths pray for his son's physical health, as he did repeatedly down the years, without praying for his health of soul. William, as an only child much at home, also received the undivided attention of both his loving parents in Christian instruction. Their united desire is to see him born again and a member of the church. His father in particular looked for evidences of the Spirit's work in his heart even from his early years, as he was sure that conversion could be real and discernible even then. After returning home after his illness, William considers joining the church, and what his father writes may strike a chord with ministers and parents, and with candidates for confirmation or even ordination. "My mind is daily exercised about my only son who is now at home, and has some thoughts of coming forward to join the church – this is a great joy to me in one sense, and seems to be an answer to many prayers – still I rejoice with trembling for fear the work in him is not a spiritual quickening – he is not forward himself, though desirous to join, if we think proper, the least objection would be enough to keep him back, as he says he is not satisfied with himself that he is in a converted state – hence my difficulty – I have nothing better to do than cast all upon God's infinite love and mercy, and try to be faithful. I was not satisfied of my own conversion when I joined the church of God, nor would I have ventured then to join, had not others pressed it on me as they believed it my duty – in looking back I am thankful to this day that I was enabled to do so, and now believe it was the Lord's will – O that it may be the same in the case of my dear and only child – I have given him to the Lord from his birth and hope He will accept the gift." In eight days' time he writes, "This forenoon we had our monthly church meeting before the Lord's Supper – I had the *pleasure of receiving my own son and only child* a full member into our church. May the Lord sanction in heaven what we did on earth in this instance . . . he answered the questions put to him with modesty and feeling – I rejoiced to see him one of the flock – still I rejoice with trembling – well knowing the many snares and difficulties that will lay in his way to honour his profession and maintain his ground – but where the Spirit of the Lord is, there is liberty and there is victory." On the Sunday following, "I had the pleasure of administering the Lord's Supper to my only child for the first time, but a considerable drawback is that his dear Mother is all day confined to her bed with alarming sickness. I want to see in himself a fuller development of the Spirit's work – I don't know how much he feels inwardly because he is naturally shy and backward in communicating his thoughts to me."

Some of the most tender and moving passages in all the diaries are prompted by that sickness of his wife, and his concern for his son's welfare and future prospects. These are proof, if any proof were needed, that strict Calvinism can go hand in hand with tender love.

Much more could be said, both light-hearted and serious. Gower Presbyterian hospitality is a byword, and perhaps goes back to the "plumb [*sic*] cakes" provided for a joint Sunday School gathering in Burry Green – no less than three hundred and ten! Then there was the dread news that a strange "murrain" had affected the potatoes, and subsequent prayer for the poor in Ireland and Scotland who "depended more on potatoes" than people in corn-growing Gower.

Times have changed; the only hope many had of seeing a doctor, or receiving medicine, was Lady Barham's bounty. Having just received a Swansea doctor's bill of one hundred pounds for a year's services to the poor, Lady Barham receives yet another request from a young girl whose mother is very ill. "The doctor, the doctor!" exclaims the noble lady. "What did you do before I came?" "Please, my lady, we died." Pen and ink were immediately called for, and the necessary chit handed over. The concern that brought Bibles, Testaments and Thomas Charles's Catechisms into Gower extended to people's physical welfare, too. In our day, people's physical health is largely the concern of the State, and their spiritual welfare that of the Church – but how weak and ailing we see the Church to be generally, including our own beloved Calvinistic Methodist or Presbyterian Church of Wales. For long years, William Griffiths felt the same about the churches of Gower. May his urgent prayer also be ours: "O for an increase in faith to labour in hope, and look beyond the deadness that prevails over the churches."

A CHRONOLOGY

1788   William Griffiths is born.

1802   Leaves home to work on local farms.

1804   His parents die.

1807   Balloted to join the Militia – stationed in Devonport, Bristol (where he joins the Welsh Chapel in Broadmead) Milford Haven, Sunderland, Newcastle, Durham and Manchester, where he was demobilised in 1812. Good training for walking the length and breadth of Gower, and beyond.

1813   Teacher.

1814   Recognised as a preacher in his county.
Lady Barham resides in Fairy Hill, and her Burry Green Chapel opened.

1815   Rees Jones appointed a preacher in Lady Barham's service in Pen-clawdd and further afield in Gower.

1816   Trinity, Cheriton, built as a school and meeting house.
Appointed a preacher by the Association, and asked to go to Pen-clawdd to assist Rees Jones in response to Lady Barham's further request.

1817   To Pen-clawdd, and then to Cheriton 'on a temporary basis'.

1818   Bethel, Pen-clawdd opened; Paraclete, Newton, built. Rees Jones ordained in Llangeitho.

1821   To Pilton Green. Lady Barham breaks with the Calvinistic Methodists, and her secretary, William Hammerton, is ordained in Burry Green Chapel by Independent Ministers.
Immanuel, Pilton Green built in three months.

1822   Association in Swansea – "Lady Barham's cause to be regarded in the same way as the Countess of Huntingdon's Connexion".
Mount Pisgah, Parkmill built.
In December, William Griffiths is given 3 months notice.

1823   New C.M. Society formed and based on Old Walls Chapel.
"No just cause of offence to be given to Lady Barham's Chapels."
Lady Barham dies, and her son, Lord Barham, inherits Cheriton and Burry Green Chapels.
First Communion Service in Old Walls Chapel, conducted by the Rev. David Charles, Carmarthen, on July 27th.

1824   William Griffiths ordained in August at Llangeitho.

In December he becomes resident minister in Burry Green under the patronage of Lord Barham, who fully recognizes that he is a minister of the Calvinistic Methodists.

1826 Marries Miss Alicia Gratiana Jones of Talley.

1828 Their only child William is born.

1836 Tabernacle, Pen-clawdd, built.

1837 Lord Barham withdraws his patronage, but allows the use of the chapels to the minister and congregations after prolonged negotiation. The local clergyman is now his brother-in-law.

1855 Lord Barham, now Earl of Gainsborough, gives the chapels at William Griffiths's request to the Calvinistic Methodists.

1860 Lewis Price becomes assistant minister.

1861 William Griffiths dies, his last sermon being preached a few weeks before from the vestry door.

1865 Mrs. Alicia Gratiana Griffiths dies at her son's home in Aberaeron, and is buried in Burry Green.

SOURCES

This paper, delivered as the Revival Memorial Lecture of the Presbyterian Church of Wales in 1997, was published in the Church's Historical Society *Journal*, 21 (1997), 66-91. It is reproduced here by kind permission of the Society.

William Griffiths Documents, National Library of Wales.
William Griffiths, Apostle of Gower – Rev. Wm. Williams.
Gower Memories (based on William Griffiths's brief account of his life) by Miss Alicia Gratiana Gower Jones, a grand-daughter.
Burry Green 150th Anniversary Brochure – B. Tudor Lloyd.
John Hughes, *Methodistiaeth Cymru*, Tair cyfrol, Gwrecsam, 1851, 1854, 1856.

Appendix 2 :
Various activities of William Griffiths

(1) Sermons at Association Meetings
(From John Robinson, *Can Mlynedd o Gymdeithasfaoedd o 1799 hyd 1899*, Caernarfon, 1900)

Date	Place	Text
6 July 1825	Carmarthen	Hosea 7:9
28 June 1827	Carmarthen	[no text given]
26 March 1828	Fishguard	Job 22:21
9 June 1829	Carmarthen	Colossians 1:28
6 July 1830	Llangadog	Psalm 136:23
7 August 1832	Llangeitho	Hebrews 11:6
8 July 1835	Llandeilo	Luke 7:35
18 May 1836	Trefin, Pembrokeshire	John 18:23
12 April 1838	Cardiff	[no text given]
2 April 1841	Neath	Luke 10:42
21 May 1841	Brecon	Revelation 21:7
29 June 1841	Llangadog	John 17:17
6 August 1846	Llandovery	Romans 11:36
10 September 1851	Caernarfon	Ephesians 5:8

(2) Welsh articles by William Griffiths in *Y Cylchgrawn* published from 1851 in Swansea by the Revs. W. Williams (Swansea) and J. Howells (Pen-coed).

Reference	Title	Text
January 1851: 12-14	What Israel must do	1 Chron. 12:32
September 1851: 169-171	The tree of life	Rev. 22:2
February 1852: 33-37	The new creature	2 Cor. 5: 17
April 1852: 97-102	A good conscience	Heb. 13:18

September 1852: 257-261	The saints' meditation on God	Ps. 104:34
January 1853: 1-5	Death	Jer. 28:16
May 1853: 129-134	Let us go on to perfection	Heb. 6:1
October 1853: 289-294	Continuing instant in prayer	Rom. 12:12
January 1854: 1-6	The unity of the Spirit in Christ's Church	Eph. 4:3
April 1854: 105-106	A good name	Eccl. 7:1
December 1854: 357-360	The cloud of witnesses	Heb. 12:1
March 1855: 69-74	Christ's government	Isa. 9:6

(3) Welsh articles by William Griffiths in Y Drysorfa

Reference	Title	Text
August 1846: 233-6	The need to know our spirit	Luke 9:55
March 1847: 76-9	Purity of mind	2 Peter 3:1
May 1847: 135-8	Humility	1 Peter 5:5
July 1847: 201-05	Evangelical obedience	Rom 16:19
December 1847: 367-71	Self-denial	Mat. 16:24
April 1848: 114-17	Christ is precious	1 Peter 2:7
December 1848: 376-80	The peace of God	Isaiah 26:12
January/February 1849: 8-10, 39-40	Spiritual comfort	Ps. 119:50
May/July 1849: 136-8, 206-210	True and false worship	John 4:22
January/February 1850: 4-5, 37-8	Lay hold of eternal life	1 Tim. 6:12
Nov/Dec 1850: 296-9, 330-32	Esteeming each other highly	Phil. 2:3
February 1851: 42-5	Sympathy	Ps. 141:5

July 1851: 229-31	Unbelief	Heb. 3:12
December 1851: 411-13	To know Christ	Phil. 3:10
May 1852: 150-52	Forgiveness	Heb. 9:22
February 1853: 37-41	The triumph of faith over the world	1 Jn. 5:4
April 1854: 109-14	Hope	Rom. 8:24
January 1855: 1-5	Christ's yoke easy	Mat. 11:30
September 1855: 290-3	Reflections on Methodistiaeth Cymru	Zech. 1:5
December 1855: 400-403	The fulness of the Spirit in the Church	Eph. 5:18
March 1856: 77-82	The value of the soul	Mat. 16:26
August 1856: 257-61	The Christian's security	Ps. 91:1
November 1856: 370-4	The mature Christian's longing	Phil. 1:23
April 1857: 109-13	The renewal of spiritual power	Isaiah 40:31
September 1857: 293-7	Family religion	Josh. 24:15
November 1857: 363-8	A large heart for religion	Ps. 119:32
October 1858: 327-30	Feasting in the service of God	John 4:32
July 1859: 221-4	The shining Christian	Phil. 2:15
December 1859: 403-07	The useful Christian	Eph. 4:16
July 1860: 228-31	Religious faithfulness	Rev. 2:10
December 1860: 412-15	The saints abiding in Christ	John 15:5
September, 1861: 298-301	Sowing and reaping	2 Cor. 9:6